ADDITIONAL PRAISE

"I have known Todd for over 15 years, and his passion, energy, enthusiasm, and spirit are truly unique. When it comes to training your body, mind, and spirit, Todd has the ability to help coach and inspire you to be your absolute best. Read his book, and it will undoubtedly help you create WOW in all areas of your life."

MILES MCPHERSON
Senior Pastor, Rock Church (San Diego, CA)

Todd isn't just the greatest strength coach in the world—he is the most complete mind and body transformer there is. To be a champion it takes so much more than just physical preparation. Todd has a knack for helping his clients/athletes reach their personal goals through his unmatched wisdom, knowledge, and energy. Todd has impacted my life, and he will impact yours too. Read this book!

MICHAEL CHANDLER
MMA World Champion

"I have known Todd for over 20 years now and have watched and witnessed his growth from a start-up in year 2000 to now dazzling crowds of all sizes. His new The WOW Book epitomizes the man he is. He's full of genuine compassion, unbridled energy, and he's the real deal. What you see on TV, on stage, and behind stage is ALL the same—a man driven by passion and purpose. If you are ready for WOW in your own life, let "Coach" guide you, motivate you, and inspire you to be your BEST. He does that to me, and he will do it for you!!"

WAYNE COTTON
CEO, Cotton Systems Ltd.

"Todd Durkin is one of the most impressive people I know. He has an amazing ability to bring out the best in people—physically, mentally, and emotionally—through constant positive encouragement. His energy and positivity are unparalleled, and he truly makes me strive to be my best. Every week I look forward to receiving TD's WOW and finding a way to apply his message to my life. I am extremely grateful to call him a friend and mentor in my life!"

CHRIS YOUNG
MLB Pitcher

"I have known Todd for more than a decade, and no one has done more for the TRX community. There is NOBODY that can fire up a crowd better than TD! His real genius is his boundless optimism and total sincerity. He's the real deal and a master motivator. His The WOW Book will light a spark under your backside!"

RANDY HETRICK
Founder & CEO, TRX

"Todd ignited the crowd at my conference last year and really WOW'd them. His talk kindled their spirit and no doubt got their mind right. The WOW Book will do the same for you."

CAROLYN CROWLEY
President, Myriad Software

"After reading Todd's IMPACT Body Plan book, I knew we needed to bring Todd in to deliver his IMPACT Leadership Program. IMPACT Leadership brought solid focus to our core values and challenged all our leaders to create WOW in their lives. His new book, The WOW Book, is a must-read if you're looking to increase motivation and take action in your professional and personal life. Todd's energy and insight is beyond impactful. It's life-changing."

HOWARD L. BIRCH
President, Quest Ventures Southwest, Inc.

"I've worked with Todd for 11 years now and I'm always amazed at how he brings WOW to all he does. His newest book is no different. If you need motivation, inspiration, or strength in any of your area of your life, Todd's 52 powerful doses will ignite you to be your absolute best. Read this book and I guarantee it will impact you positively!"

JULIE WILCOX
GM, Fitness Quest 10

"For the past 9 years, I have chosen to train with Todd Durkin. He has helped me in all aspects of football and life and I love his positivity, mindset, and energy that he brings to all he does. His training and coaching has helped me reach many milestones in my career and he has made me a better human being. Read his new WOW book and I know it will help you also!"

DARREN SPROLES
RB, Philadelphia Eagles, 2-Time Pro Bowl Player

"People often ask me how I stay in such peak condition. They also ask where I learned the mindset and discipline it takes to stick to my healthy lifestyle. And I give them 2 words, TODD DURKIN!! I've been flying across the country from east to west coast for 6 years to train with Todd because the first time I encountered him he impacted my life that much…and he still does to this day. If you want to change your life for the better… READ THIS BOOK!!

GERALD MCCOY
DL, Tampa Bay Buccaneers, 4-Time Pro Bowl Player

"When you talk about being great, you have to be immersed in an environment that allows you to excel. Excellence is in the details and I train with Todd because he gets into ALL aspects of your training and life. And his new WOW Book is no different."

ZACH ERTZ
TE, Philadelphia Eagles

"I've been around Todd my entire 9-year professional football career and I can promise you there's no better coach, friend or mentor out there. His words will change your life."

CHASE DANIEL
QB, Philadelphia Eagles

52 Ways to Motivate Your Mind, Inspire Your Soul & Create WOW in Your Life!

THE
WOW
BOOK

TODD DURKIN

Author of The IMPACT Body Plan,
Performance Coach & Master Motivator

Todd Durkin Enterprises
9972 Scripps Ranch Blvd.
San Diego, CA 92131

www.ToddDurkin.com

Printed in the United States of America

First Printing, 2016

ISBN 978-1537780603

DEDICATION

To Larry Indiviglia

You gave me the idea to start doing our "Word of the Week" (WOWs) way back in October 2011. And over the years it grew into a whole lot more. It became a ritual. A theme. A focus. And now, a book.

As my main "wingman" in all I do, I am grateful for your service, friendship, and kindred spirit. You truly are one of the finest human beings on the planet, and I am blessed to rub elbows with you every day between Fitness Quest 10, the Mastermind, filming projects, special projects, workouts, and all that you do. I am blessed to have someone like you in my life.

If there were 7 (your favorite number) words that I would use to describe you, they would be: caring, compassionate, coach, leader, empathetic, loving, and friend.

I dedicate this book to you, brother. Thanks for making me a better human being. You epitomize the word "WOW!"

(L/R: Todd Durkin, Larry Indiviglia)

CONTENTS

FOREWORD

I was a graduate student in exercise and nutrition science at San Diego State University in 1997 when I first met Todd Durkin. I can remember the exact moment in time that he came up and introduced himself. What I remember most was his positive energy and sparkling eyes. I knew I wanted to get to know him better, and we became close friends that first year—before it turned into so much more! We studied together, worked out together, and enjoyed a carefree time before kids and careers took hold.

Three years after we started dating was the happiest day of my life, our wedding day—February 17, 2001. We opened Fitness Quest 10 the year before, and I was one year into my position as a college professor at Southwestern College in Chula Vista, California. Looking back, a lot has changed for both of us in terms of responsibilities and time restraints, but 15 years later and we still collaborate a ton in our fitness fields, love our Fitness Quest 10 family, and, in addition to our three children, have created an amazing circle of people who mean so much to us and make life worth living.

When people who know and love Todd meet me, a few of the same questions tend to come up:

"Is he always so **energetic**?" and "How does he stay so **motivated**?"

I have been answering these questions for a long time now, and it always makes me smile when I consider Todd's incredibly positive image with the community he reaches and with the people who follow him. The answer to the questions—Todd is **honestly** an **energetic** and **motivating** guy. He is **genuine** in his ability to be

positive and **uplifting**, and he certainly has more energy than the average person!

Even still, I know the Todd who needs to recharge his batteries and decompress after firing up and motivating fitness pros or business executives over the course of a single-day or multiple-day event. That Todd exists too!

Because Todd is a **natural** at what he does and he does it so well, I totally understand how people might assume he is always as he appears on video or on stage.

To have a backstage view into how Todd maintains his ability to **motivate** and **inspire** so many people each week and each day has been one of the greatest blessings in my life. To watch his work ethic and commitment to his mission of inspiring millions to strive for **1% better every day** and make **big impact** in their lives is not something I take for granted.

I am always so happy to meet Todd's fans and friends from all over the globe, and deep down it fills me with pride to see how Todd has worked and persisted at becoming a **master motivator** who makes a huge difference in so many lives.

Todd's **genuine** ability to connect with others and remember them, and stay connected across time is one of his true strengths. Todd was doing this before Facebook and social media even made it easier! I remember in the late 1990s (before we had social media or even email) that Todd created a reach across the country and world that was unlike anything I had seen before. He had friends across the globe and kept in touch with so many of them, and in return opened up my life to so many amazing people and lifelong friendships.

If I had to pick only two words to describe Todd, I would choose **authentic** and **enthusiastic**—in his energy levels, interest in others, his ability to connect, and, most importantly, his aim to stay connected with people across the globe.

Five years ago when Todd started writing his "word of the week"—his WOWs—so many people would tell me, "Todd's words are spot-on" or "It feels like he is talking directly to me," that I knew he was onto something special. I would come home and give Todd more and more names to add to his list. I sat back and watched that WOW list grow and grow over the years.

Todd never missed a week of writing a new WOW for years. The practice of creating, writing, and sending a WOW message each week for five **consistent** years is an example of the **commitment** Todd has to his message of **motivating** and **inspiring** people to reach their **full potential**.

In 2014, when we took a family dream vacation to Europe, those were the first two weeks that Todd had planned into his calendar that didn't include writing WOWs. (Coincidently, it was in that time on our family vacation to Europe that the inspiration for creating this book came about.)

Todd & Melanie in Lake Garda, Italy

As impressed as I became with how large his list and reach were with people receiving the weekly WOWs, deep down I knew that it wasn't close to the amount of people who would love to be part of that list and part of Todd's community. The idea to compile the weekly WOWs into a book to share with many more people was my idea, but only because I truly am Todd's biggest supporter and I believe in Todd's gift of teaching us to **think more deeply, believe** in ourselves, and access our most **hopeful, positive,** and **strong** selves. And I hope this WOW book maximizes the number of people experiencing this gift of **deep self-belief** and **aspiration**.

I know you will enjoy getting to know Todd through these WOW stories and find inspiration in his words. He truly is **genuine** in his writing and his **belief** that you can make your life **better** and more **impactful** with a shift in mindset and an openness to bringing more WOW into your life.

It is my pleasure to participate in this project of bringing WOW to all readers of this book. Todd and I conceived this book as a gesture of **love** for our special community of friends and family—and we **welcome** you now into that circle!

With love,

Melanie Durkin
Todd's wife and biggest fan

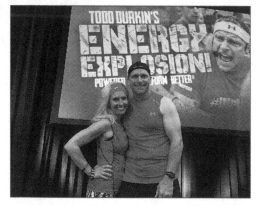

Todd & Melanie teaching at IDEA World, Los Angeles

INTRODUCTION

For the past five years, I have done something EVERY Sunday afternoon without fail. I write something called a "WOW." This stands for "word of the week."

The WOW is typically one word or one phrase that I expand into a one-page short story, garnered around a specific theme for the week. I started it in 2011 for just my Mastermind Group of personal trainers. Then I began sharing it with my team at Fitness Quest 10. Later I expanded the list to include clients and members at the gym.

And the more I shared my WOWs, the more people kept telling me how much of a difference it was making in their mindset for the day and for the week. And then more and more people asked to be added to the WOW list.

I enjoyed writing the WOWs and seeing the **impact** they were creating, and I loved the **positive** feedback I was getting on a weekly basis. So I kept writing them!

* * *

In July 2014, I was in Italy with my family for a two-week European bucket-list vacation that included England, Germany, Austria, and Italy. It was one of those once-in-a-lifetime vacations that provided truly magnificent experiences for me and my family.

At the tailend of the trip, I was driving our rental vehicle from Lake Garda, Italy, to Venice. My three kids were sleeping in the back of the SUV, and my wife, Melanie, and I were in a deep discussion about life. It was one of those talks that you just truly cherish and wish you could do more often.

Specifically, Melanie and I were talking about our dreams, our visions, our relationship, our careers, and all that we wanted out of life.

And then Melanie said something quite profound. She turned down the music and spoke in a very serious and loving voice, "Todd, it's time for you to write your next book.

"You write every week, you love it, and you need to get your message out to more people. Hundreds of people receive your WOW every week and love it.

"I think you need to write a book on WOW, a book about people being their best in life. A book that **motivates** and **inspires** people at the core of their **soul**. A book that allows people to overcome head trash, adversity, and challenge. A book that **inspires** athletes and non-athletes alike. A book that **inspires** kids and adults alike.

"And I think it needs to be a compilation of short stories and messages. It needs to be easily digestible for people and provide nuggets of **motivation** people can chew on daily. It needs to have your **soul** and your **spirit**. It needs to ignite **passion**. It needs to help people discover and live their **life's purpose**. And it ultimately needs to create **IMPACT** for people.

"It should offer all of your WOWs in one place. A book that is designed to do what you do best: **getting people's minds right!**"

There was silence.

I became overwhelmed with emotion. I literally welled up with tears and saw a vision. She was right—I needed to start writing!

* * *

In your hands, you are reading the book that stemmed from the idea of my wife, Melanie, born on a two-hour car ride on a hot summer day in Italy.

And while I have been writing a WOW every week for many years now for a select list of people, I never thought about compiling my WOWs into a book for ALL people who want to **get their minds right**.

In this book, you now have 52 WOWS to read. Each of these WOWs has a theme. You can read them once a week for a year, making the particular WOW theme into your week's focus. Or you can read one a day for 52 days straight.

The WOW Book is meant to be read over and over again. I want you to go back and reread the stories that MOST resonate with your **spirit**. Mark the book up. Underline key phrases. Circle things. Make notes. Write down things that come to mind.

At the end of each WOW, I give an "Action Step" that includes questions or suggestions, so you can apply that WOW to your day, your week—your LIFE. I recommend buying a special notebook or journal—we can call it your "WOW journal." Use that journal as a space to react, explore, and respond to the WOWs. Use it as a space to **get your mind right**.

You'll also notice that I've made a website, www.ToddDurkin.com/WOWbook-Resources, to share additional resources so that you have even more options for creating WOW in your life. You'll even find 8 additional "**And Then Some . . . WOWS**" on the site to give you that extra support on your journey of WOW, as well as suggested workouts, guided meditations, short videos, pictures, and more.

And that's the aim of this project—to help YOU create **WOW** and **get your mind right**.

Share or gift *The WOW Book* with others. **Share** it with your kids. Your co-workers. Your clients. Your family. After all, the more each of us strives with **conviction** and **inspiration** to live our **BEST**, the better life will be. And the more **WOW** that will be created by all.

And as always, **commit** to training hard, eating right, and living inspired. I'm confident this book will help you do all these things.

My friends, it's time to **GET YOUR MIND RIGHT**, and it's time to create **WOW**. And it starts right now!

WOW 1

TIME

When I was in college in 1992, email did not exist. Imagine that.

So if you wanted to drop someone a note, you literally had to put it in the mail, and it would get there a few days later.

And every single day while I was at William & Mary in Virginia, for 3.5 years, I would get a letter in my mailbox from my father. Every. Single. Day.

Now imagine that. Imagine receiving a handwritten note every single day from someone you love. Some notes were longer than others. Some were even on the back of McDonald's menus. Most had newspaper clippings from my New Jersey hometown paper, *Asbury Park Press*, on local sporting news.

And all of them used to make me smile. And feel so loved.

Heck, imagine writing a handwritten letter nowadays. And clipping articles. And driving to the post office. Imagine doing that once a month. Or every week. Or even—every single day. Wow.

But then it stopped one day.

I received a phone call in February 1992 that my dad was having a heart attack. Because I immediately flew home that day, I was able to see Dad alive, one last time in the hospital.

And then he died. February 19, 1992. Fifty-eight years old.

I was devastated. Dad was everything to me. For twenty years, he was my friend. My father. My life coach. And my mentor.

And now he was gone.

It was undoubtedly the toughest challenge I had ever faced in my life. I never lost anyone that close in my life. Let alone my mentor. Let alone a parent.

For several weeks, I stayed at home and grieved.

I remember crying every night.

I remember early-morning runs on the beach in Bay Head in the bone-chilling cold of New Jersey, just crying as I was running.

I remember long drives around the Shore to visit places we would visit together. The inlet at Point Pleasant. The football stadium at Brick High School. The Great Auditorium in Ocean Grove.

I would just sit at these places where I had such fond memories of times with my dad—and cry. And cry. And cry some more.

And I would contemplate life's plan. My future. My faith. My purpose. And it was downright scary to face this without Dad.

Three weeks after my dad's death, I heard his voice tell me something, "Get up, dust yourself off, get back to school, and I will be there with you."

So, that's what I did.

And one of the most amazing things happened as soon as I returned.

Guess where I went?

To retrieve my mail at my postbox.

And what was in there?

A letter written from my father on the day before he died. I just hadn't received it yet.

And this letter just happened to be one of the deepest, longest, most profound letters I EVER received from him. It was all about my future.

It talked about our family. It talked about Mom. It talked about my seven brothers and sisters. And it talked about me. My father told me—

It doesn't matter what you do in life, as long as you are happy. Whether it be a teacher and coach. A doctor. A politician. An athlete. A businessman. Whatever you choose to do, do it with all your heart and might, make a difference in people's lives, and be happy.

WOW.

And he said one more thing—

*Remember that life is very precious and **TIME** is the most important asset we all have. Be sure to use it wisely. I will always love you regardless of WHAT you do. It's WHO you become that's most important. Love, Dad.*

That was it.

I remember reading this letter from my dad in the campus post office, with tears running down my face. And it felt incredibly warm to be receiving this note at that time—like he was with me.

As I write this now, with tears running down my face, I can't help but think of the impact he had on me.

He was my friend. My biggest fan. My coach. My mentor. My father. And I would be remiss if I didn't start my *WOW* book with the person who had the greatest IMPACT on me.

After all, WHY WAIT to share my best lessons until later in the book?

ACTION STEP

Think of the one person in your life who is closest to you. The person whom you would LEAST like to have taken away from you. Who is that person? Write it down in a journal.

And now, do two things—

First, make sure that person knows how much you admire, love, and respect them.

And second, most importantly, go out and spend quality time with that person as soon as possible.

After all, **TIME** is the most important asset we all have.

Thanks, Dad. I'm glad you taught me such an important lesson that I can pass along today.

WOW 2
LABOR

One of the men that's had the greatest impact on me besides my father is Coach Warren Wolf. He is a high school football coaching legend. Literally. He was like a god for any young man that wanted to play high school football. Not only was he highly acclaimed on the Jersey Shore and all of New Jersey, but also the country. Check out some of his amazing stats:

- 24 Shore Conference Championships

- 13 New Jersey State Titles

- 6th Most Winning Coach in the US—of ALL TIME

- 4th in the nation of football coaches by number of seasons coached

- 51 years as a head coach at one school (Brick, New Jersey)

He was and is a living legend. And he is a huge mentor of mine.

When I was young boy, I would dream of playing for Coach Wolf. I would stand at the edge of the fence of Keller Memorial Field and watch the "Silver Fox" lead his Green Dragons with the Michigan-type wing-tipped helmets onto the field. And I dreamt of someday running out on that same field.

My brother Paul actually quarterbacked the first New Jersey football state championship for Coach Wolf in 1974 when the undersized, undermanned Brick Green Dragons out-coached, out-disciplined, and out-hit Camden, New Jersey, 21 to 20. I was just three years old at the time, but it was the first of Coach Wolf's 13 state championships.

My opportunity to play for Coach Wolf came early as I was fortunate to start as a young freshman quarterback for his powerhouse program. I was scared. I was excited. I was nervous. I was pumped. And I did not want to let down Coach Wolf.

And over a four-year high school career that eventually led to a football scholarship to William & Mary, I learned a ton of extremely valuable lessons from Coach Wolf that still apply today.

But the best one came on **LABOR** Day before my senior year in 1988.

And it goes like this:

It was Labor Day weekend (fall 1988) at Brick Township High School in New Jersey, and we were just starting our football practice. It was about 9 am, 90 degrees, humid, and a holiday. It was **LABOR** Day.

After doing some light calisthenics and drills for about ten minutes, the venerable Coach Wolf blew his whistle about seven times in the same rhythm and fashion that always signified the END of practice.

As the 90 players or so rushed into the middle of the field, our immediate thoughts were "Could he be cancelling the rest of practice and letting us out early because of the **Labor** Day holiday?"

As we were all smiling, laughing, and preparing for the great news, Coach Wolf in his ever-present black high-top cleats, long shorts, white t-shirt, long-brimmed floppy hat, and raspy voice began to speak.

"Boys. You've been working hard. Real hard. And today is a holiday. It's **LABOR** DAY. I know you want a championship, and it takes a lot of hard work to be the best. So I have made a decision."

We all looked at each other with excitement about to sprint off the field in exuberance, awaiting the good news of practice being let out early.

"Boys. You've been working hard . . . real hard. And I know you are trying to build a championship. And championships don't come easy. Hard work doesn't take holidays. Championships aren't built on taking days off. And we have a championship to build. Because it's L-A-A-B-O-O-R-R-R Day . . . that's what we are going to do today . . . LABOR!!! LABOR, LABOR, L-A-A-A-A-B-B-B-B-O-O-O-R-R-R-R. It's time to **LABOR**!!!!"

And labor we did. Two-and-a-half hours of Jersey, hazy, hot humidity on a holiday weekend.

I share this story for several reasons. One, it still sticks with me twenty-five-plus years later. I can still see myself as a young seventeen-year-old quarterback looking up at coach with the wide-eyed enthusiasm of a ten-year-old. I respected Coach Wolf for my entire life, and he has always served as a mentor.

The other reason is because we did win a championship that season, and it was built on the same principles that Coach Wolf practiced and preached —even on **LABOR** DAY: hard work, practice, repetition, mental toughness, and discipline, even when you don't feel like it.

These were just some of the things that made us successful that year . . . and made us champions.

Coach Wolf IMPACTED thousands of young men in his 52-year coaching career. I was just one of many.

Perhaps he taught me the greatest lesson of all: you always have to **LABOR** if you want to be great . . . even on **LABOR** DAY. ☺

ACTION STEP

What do you need to "labor" on today? Maybe you are tired. Maybe you are about to give up. Or maybe it's even a holiday. What's ONE THING you can do today to get one step closer to getting to where you want to go?

Now go do it.

Thank you, Coach Wolf. You taught me a lot about how to live. How to not only be a better football player but a more solid citizen. A stronger leader. A man of faith. A husband and a father. A better person. And a better laborer.

Now get to work!

WOW 3
DO BETTER!

Ken Sawyer was my best friend. He was one of my biggest cheerleaders. And he was a great human being.

And he is no longer here.

Ken was a client of mine for seventeen years. He rarely missed my boot camps on Saturday mornings. I trained him during the week. He was my insurance agent. He was an amazing husband and incredible father to two children. He was the best friend anyone could ever ask for.

And he died on June 26, 2012.

On a Tuesday morning at 6 am, Ken was driving his motor scooter to meet a friend for an early-morning run and was hit by a car. Ken was only fifty-one years old.

I could go on and on about the amazing man that Ken was. Or share the goofy, funny things he used to say. Or how inviting Ken was to every new attendee at a Saturday morning boot camp class. Or how he loved to playfully haze our fitness interns every Saturday. Or share how he would go out of his way for ANY of his friends in need at any time of the day, literally, to lend a helping hand or be an ear to talk to.

There was no one like Ken Sawyer.

And he taught me a lot of lessons. I want to share one of those lessons with you today.

In 1999, I was looking for space to open my training studio. And I thought I found a little space. It was about 600 square feet, and I actually kind of fell in love with it. I envisioned my studio there with simple, functional exercise equipment and a massage table to do my bodywork. I was convinced that this was the next step for me.

The overhead was low. It was close to where I was living at the time. And it seemed like a logical next step.

Then I shared my vision with Ken. And he vehemently disagreed with me.

Ken urged, "Todd, you can **DO BETTER** than that. This place is too small. You need bigger. Listen, NOW is the time for you in your life to take big risks."

And I countered, "Ken, I can't afford to take RISKS right now."

He responded, "Bull crap. You have nothing to lose. You don't own a home. You barely own a car. You're not married. You have very little money. And you have very little assets. Now is the perfect time to take a BIG risk. You have nothing to lose . . . literally!"

Well, that certainly didn't make me feel too good . . .

But he was right—I had nothing to lose. Why NOT go for my dream place NOW?

Six months later, I found that dream location and opened my 2,000 square foot studio, Fitness Quest 10, in an area of San Diego called Scripps Ranch. And the rest is history.

There were many a day after I opened Fitness Quest 10 that Ken would come up and joke to me about how he wished I'd only opened that "one-room closet" to train one person at a time. And he would just laugh and laugh, as people were bustling all over the place and practically tripping over each other.

After multiple expansions and much growth of Fitness Quest 10,

Ken and I would often reflect about life and how you need to live life to its fullest . . . NOW and not wait.

Pretty interesting that after Ken's tragic death, I found a yellow sticky note taped to his computer screen that said the following words: **DO BETTER!!**

Do better. Think about that. *Do better*.

How can you **DO BETTER**?

- Maybe it's in your business.

- Or the leadership of your team.

- Or communication with your spouse.

- Or being present with your kids and not on your phone when you're around them.

- Or being laser-focused on what you NEED to be doing with your life. You know, not getting so distracted with "unimportant" things.

- Maybe it's in your physical conditioning. Or your nutrition.

- Maybe it's finally doing what you have been saying you're going to do for the past few months. Or years.

To me, the mindset and lesson that I learned from Ken is that we can always **DO BETTER**. I use the mantra "1% Better Every Day" as a daily reminder on my continual improvement.

What is the **ONE THING** you can do today to get **1% BETTER**?

> ### 🏃 ACTION STEP
>
> Define and write down how you can **DO BETTER** in your own life. And then share it with someone.
>
> And then go out and **DO IT . . . BETTER!!!**

Oh yeah, call up or email a mentor and let them know the **IMPACT** they have had in your life. You just never know when it's going to be too late to let them know the difference they made.

We all have 8,720 hours in a year. That is exactly 525,600 minutes. And it's up to YOU as to what you do with your time.

Maximize every minute you have and always choose to **DO BETTER**!

Thank you, Ken, for being in my life for seventeen years. And while you are sorely missed by so many today, I can assure you that your life's message and lesson to **DO BETTER** will never die. Thanks, brother, for continuing to inspire me to **DO BETTER**.

WOW 4
SPIRIT & MTXE

One of the best coaches in college basketball history is Steve Fisher. He won a national championship at the University of Michigan in 1989. He has been coaching at San Diego State University since 2000. He has amassed over 375 wins in his career. Quite impressive.

In 2014, I got the unique opportunity to be a "special guest coach" on the sidelines with Coach Steve Fisher and the San Diego State University Aztecs on game day against UNLV.

As a guest coach, I went to the shoot around at 2 pm, and Coach Fisher introduced me to the team. At 3 pm, when we were having our "pre-game" meal with the team, I sat with Coach Fisher and asked him a few questions (remember, whenever you are in the presence of a GREAT coach, be sure to ask a few "deep" questions).

One of the questions I asked Coach Fisher was "Who was your favorite coach of all time, and was there one coach who you emulated your style after?"

Without hesitation, he responded, "John Wooden."

And I asked WHY.

Coach Fisher said several things about him. One being that Coach Wooden was a great man who often talked about how PRACTICE was the most essential part to winning when it came to game day. Yeah, practice, we talkin' practice. (Thank you, Allen Iverson.)

He talked of Wooden's character. His values. His legacy. The way he treated all his players. (You can read about Coach Wooden in WOW 11 LOVE.)

Thirty minutes prior to the game and right before warm-ups, Coach Fisher and his standout assistants went over the final scouting report and had an in-depth analysis on every player from UNLV. It was pretty impressive and showed they obviously were prepared.

And then twelve minutes before tip-off, Coach Fisher brought the team (including me) into the locker room for final instructions.

It was there that I was excited to hear how he addressed his team. Was he an emotional leader? An inspirational man? Soft-spoken?

I would say that Coach Fisher was a bit of all of it. He was very "fatherly" as he spoke. He had motivation, conviction, heart, and compassion—all wrapped into one.

He spoke of six keys to the game:

- Poise under pressure

- Controlled emotion

- Supreme confidence

- Expect success

- MTXE

- Togetherness

I loved how he spoke about "Expect success" and how you need to go to bed at night dreaming of "cutting down the nets." That resonated deeply.

But I really loved **MTXE**—*mental toughness, x-tra effort*. He said this has been a mantra of his for years.

Mental Toughness.

Extra Effort.

Tough under fire. Tough under duress. Tough when challenged.

And extra effort. This is the 1% difference. The "getting better every day" mentality it takes to be a champion. The "and then some" attitude to be the best.

MTXE. I LOVE IT.

*   *   *

SDSU was getting their butts beat in the first half. The 15th ranked team in the country played one of the worst first halves of their season. So I was curious to see how Coach Fisher would address his team at the half.

Instead of yelling, ranting, and raving, he had everyone take a nice deep breath and settle down. He told the guys to relax, close their eyes, and envision how they wanted the second half to go.

He and his staff gave a few pointers on offense, a few on defense, and touched upon the mental approach to the second half.

The team went out and played a great second half. Really hammering out that mental toughness and extra effort Coach Fisher was talking about. Despite getting out-rebounded and "out-bigged," they hung tough until the end.

They lost in the closing moments in a very exciting game. And it was a great experience.

Someone remarked the following day, "It's too bad they lost."

And instead of replying, "I know," I responded a bit differently:

"You know, I really wanted the Aztecs to win that game. It was really cool being in the locker room, being in the huddle at every timeout, and really hearing the Xs and Os of the game. And to hear it when they weren't playing well and playing such a formidable opponent made it even more special.

"But what was most impressive about the game was to see how Coach Fisher handled his players when things were *not* going well. In a game where they didn't have their best or play their best."

That to me was incredible. To see how a great coach handled his team during timeouts and in the locker room when they were frazzled or down was truly a special experience. And to hear how he addressed his team after the hard-fought loss was special.

If there was one word that I had to describe Coach Fisher, it is this: **SPIRIT**. There was a time during the game when one of his players made an incredible play and dunk. And Coach Fisher turned to his bench, looked at his players, and just had this incredibly proud smile on his face. It truly was filled with great **spirit**.

It was striking to see the reverence his team had for him when he was saying (as he would often say before he started to speak to his team), "Give me your eyes and ears." Coach Fisher had tremendous **spirit**, and all his players recognized it too.

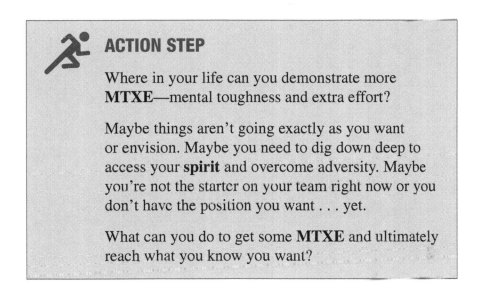

ACTION STEP

Where in your life can you demonstrate more **MTXE**—mental toughness and extra effort?

Maybe things aren't going exactly as you want or envision. Maybe you need to dig down deep to access your **spirit** and overcome adversity. Maybe you're not the starter on your team right now or you don't have the position you want . . . yet.

What can you do to get some **MTXE** and ultimately reach what you know you want?

Thanks, Coach Fisher. You taught me a lot that night. Your **SPIRIT** was inspiring, and **MTXE** always matters!

WOW 5

GUTS

 Sometimes you just know "in your gut" what is right and what is wrong. Sometimes you just get a feel for what you are supposed to do in a certain situation.

When I was in college, I was a government major. And then I changed to business.

And I was miserable.

It was then that I got some of the best advice I've ever received.

My sister Patti, the oldest of my five sisters, told me something that changed the course of my life.

Patti advised me, "You need to **listen to your gut**. What does your intuition say? What do you most love studying? What do you most enjoy?"

I thought about that for a minute and knew that I loved this intro to kinesiology class I was taking.

But I was already a junior, so I'd been thinking, "It's probably too late for me to change majors this late in the game."

And then I started building in more excuses, "If I changed my major to PE/kinesiology, that's really going to limit my career choices." (You've got to remember, there weren't quite the career options within kinesiology/exercise science in 1991 as there are today.)

And then Patti said something else even more profound, "Listen to your heart. It rarely leads you wrong. Trust your internal voice and follow your passion. Don't worry about money and career choices. That will come as a result of you ultimately discovering your true passion and having the courage to blaze your own path . . . and that all starts with **TRUSTING YOUR GUT**."

That's it. That's all I needed to hear.

As a junior at William & Mary in 1991, I changed my major to Kinesiology. And I fell in love with it. I found my passion. And my soul was singing.

I ended up getting my degree on time in 1993. I took a fifth year and got my PE teacher's certification as a back-up plan. I went to massage therapy school. I got my personal trainer's certification and eventually became a strength and conditioning coach. Eventually, I earned a master's degree in biomechanics and sports medicine, and took advanced workshops in bodywork and massage.

And I just couldn't get enough learning in this field of study. I studied relentlessly. I read every book I could get my hands on. I watched videotapes and DVDs. I attended live conferences and workshops. And I just kept learning and learning about all that was inside of the field of health, fitness, sports, conditioning, nutrition, bodywork, healing, alternative health, and anything related to exercise science, sport psychology, and performance.

And in 2000, I listened to my gut again. I opened my small 2,000 square foot training studio, Fitness Quest 10, in San Diego, California. It was scary as hell. I had no clients, no money, and no business plan. Then I was able to jump-start the business with my passion and knowledge.

Most importantly, it was **my gut** that told me to do it—and I listened.

And since then, a lot of good things have happened. And one of the reasons why is because of the lesson I learned from my sister Patti that I still apply today: **You gotta trust your gut**.

Nowadays, I listen to my **gut** on a lot of things:

- Hiring

- Firing

- Leadership

- Communication

- Expanding the business.

- New opportunities that arise and if I should participate in them

- Strategic growth

- Financial decisions

- And the list goes on and on . .

> **ACTION STEP**
>
> What major decisions are you making right now in your life?
>
> And what does your **gut** say about it?

Listen intently to that feeling and **trust your gut**, for your intuition rarely leads you wrong.

Become a master at listening to your "**gut instincts**," and watch how that ultimately allows you to fulfill your passion and purpose in life.

And that is **IMPACT**...and that will help you **create WOW**!

WOW 6
GET MO' IN YO' LIFE!

One of the mentors who has impacted me greatly is Pastor Miles McPherson of Rock Church, San Diego. He has that gift when preaching to make you think, "He's talking directly to me."

Many years ago he said something during a sermon that was very funny (he does that a lot) and **IMPACTFUL**.

And what he said pertains really to ALL areas of life.

Miles was talking about momentum and shared we all needed momentum in our lives.

He said, "You got to **get MO' in yo' life**! MO-MENTUM leads to **MO'** health, **MO'** money, **MO'** happiness, **MO'** harmony, **MO'** everything."

He further explained.

"All of us need **MO-MENTUM** in our life. **Momentum** in our careers. In our jobs. In getting our BHAGs (big, hairy, audacious goals) done. In our relationships. In our physical health. In our spiritual walk."

Momentum is a good thing. If you think of an athletic contest, shifts in **momentum** play a major role in the outcome of a game.

If you think of business, you've got to love when **mo-mentum** is flowing and it's going the way you envisioned it. Clients are happy.

There is a continuous influx of new clients and members enlisting in your services. Your team is thriving. The culture is thriving, and the energy is pumping. And you got that bounce in your step.

If you think of your own life, when things are going well and you are feeling strong and healthy, you become more vibrant and radiant. And you have that extra confidence and swag. And then "coincidentally" (or not), a series of good things seem to happen all in a row.

That is called **MO-MENTUM**.

And we could all use more of it in our lives.

The problem is that sometimes we get in our own way. Or we let excuses build up, and we start to have negative self-talk. And we begin saying things like:

- *Now is not the right time.*

- *I'll wait until the economy shifts.*

- *I'll wait to do that until I have x amount of money in the bank.*

- *I'm too young.*

- *I'm too old.*

- *I have too much education.*

- *I don't have enough education.*

- *I am over-qualified.*

- *I am under-qualified.*

And the excuses go on and on. And they are robbing you of YOU being the BEST version of you.

Two ways to combat excuses and negativity:

1. **Faith.** Not just faith in God but faith in yourself. I personally think they go hand in hand, but we can save that talk for another day. The point—you need faith.

2. **Take ACTION**. NOW! Say yes to what you want, even when you don't know all the answers, and you will figure it out along the way.

So if you want some serious **MO-MENTUM** in your life, now is the time to take ACTION on what you most want in life.

ACTION STEP

Define what is the biggest excuse that is currently holding you back from achieving the ONE THING you most want/need in your life right now.

Next, take ONE specific **ACTION** step that will help you overcome that excuse/fear and help you achieve your goal. And put down a date or deadline when you will take your **ACTION** step!

Instead of living by the mantra "Ready . . . AIM . . . AIM . . . AIM . . ." and never even firing, I have a different mantra I live by:

Ready . . . FIRE . . . Aim!!!

Get yourself ready, prepare like mad, and then start FIRING. That is called ACTION. And ACTION leads to MO-MENTUM.

And yes, **MO-MENTUM** will lead to **MO'** health, **MO'** money, **MO'** happiness, **MO'** harmony, and **MO'** everything.

So **get MO' in YO' life** and watch what happens.

29

WOW 7
YIN OR YANG?

Many years ago, I had a crushing injury to my back while playing football. This led me down a healing path to reconstruct my own body and rid myself of a nasty Vicodin habit. It was one of the most difficult times of my life, dealing with the physical pain, and the mental and emotional depressive state it left me in. Although I was only 25 years old at the time, this part of my life's journey was an extremely **IMPACTFUL** one.

Twenty years later, I think about how these earlier events of my life led me to what I do today. WHO I am today. Pain became part of my story. The nurse coming to my condo twice a day to shoot me up with painkillers. The bed I lay in for four weeks before being able to crutch around the streets of Cannes, France (where the injury happened), in order to go to physical therapy just a half-mile away. The Vicodin. The loss of muscle mass. The loss of my dream to play in the NFL. The fear that I might need back surgery while in another country. The fear of the unknown.

The other day I was reflecting on my injury and how it still **IMPACTS** me today. I was thinking of all the various treatments and modalities I used then and how they compare to what we do and have now.

Back then, I tried everything available to me. I really wanted to do all I could to avoid surgery on my three herniated discs, spinal stenosis, and degenerative back disease. You name it, I tried it. Acupuncture, chiropractic, osteopathy, energy medicine, physical therapy, massage therapy, visualization. And yes, painkillers. I popped the "Vike" just to manage my pain. And I did that for nine months.

Then I met my man, Dub Leigh (a gruff old man about 77 years old), who introduced me to his bodywork that he called "Zen Bodytherapy." It combined Rolfing, Feldenkrais, and energy work. Within six sessions, I had a serious detox, rid myself of my Vicodin habit (haven't popped one of those since 1996), and locked in on a new dream for my future.

Dub changed my philosophy on healing and performance training. He also changed my life.

This short journey down memory lane is a reminder to me that in some ways we are all just one step away from injury. From pain. From fear. From change. And for some, from a NEED so great we would try anything to fix the problem, including prescription drugs.

And when this happens, we FINALLY turn to others for help. Doctors. Chiropractors. Personal trainers. Physical therapists. Massage therapists. Yogis. Pilates instructors. Trainers specializing in corrective exercise. Nutritionists. Acupuncturists. The list goes on.

They were always there. Always available to us. Ready and waiting with knowledge and tools to strengthen us. To teach us how to take better care of ourselves. To prevent injury. To prevent pain. To live strong, healthy, and well.

But most of us wait for an emergency. And then we call for help. Help to heal us in body and mind. And we pray it's not too late.

You see, we live in a traditional system that is predominantly REACTIVE, but we need to be **PROACTIVE**. And so I ask—**Why wait? Why wait for a need so great?**

My friend, **LET ME SAVE YOU THE PAIN**. Read the signs. Don't wait to make a call.

- Maybe your hips are tight.

- Maybe your back is locked, and it's affecting your sleep, your energy, and your mood.

- Maybe you have sciatica pain down your leg, and it's affecting your activities of daily living.

- Maybe your range of motion is lessened due to tightness in the rotator cuff.

- Maybe you're overweight, and the excess fat is hurting your joints. Or your heart.

- Maybe you're depressed right now.

- Maybe your hormones are raging and all over the place.

My friend, **enough is enough**. Today is the first day of your new plan to **restore**, **re-energize**, and **recover**. Today you will change your direction away from injury toward wellness. *Today, you become the captain of your health and begin your plan to FEEL YOUR BEST*.

Permit me to make some professional recommendations that will help you improve your performance and everyday living. Your LIFE. These are methods, tools, and modalities that will help you live and feel extraordinary. I will cover a few in this WOW.

Note: If you are currently in a high-intensity interval training program (like the ones I often prescribe), then these restorative measures are even more important to help you recover and re-energize. Together, it's an ideal combination to help you **BE YOUR BEST**.

Yoga. It's over 2,000 years old and a great form of exercise. While there are hundreds of different types of yoga, find a flow that works for you. Hatha. Iyengar. Ashtanga (power). Bikram (hot) yoga. Vinyasa. Kundalini. While traditional forms of strength training often shorten muscle and fascia, yoga helps lengthen the fascia and restore balance. The breathwork alone is therapeutic as it calms the central nervous system. Remember, you do not need to be Gumby to do yoga. The purpose of yoga is to help you open your body, creating balance and strength.

Pilates. I love when my athletes incorporate Pilates into their program even if only once a week. Pilates provides full body conditioning to build flexibility, lengthen muscles, and strengthen the legs, abdominals, arms, hips, and back. There are some very specific, unique exercises for the feet, for ankle mobility, for hip mobility, and core strengthening. While Pilates is a great form of strength training for most, I love it for the restorative aspect as well.

Therapeutic Massage and Bodywork. Why do we wait until something hurts to get a massage? Despite hundreds of different forms of bodywork, the bottom line is that soft tissue work manipulates fascia to help restore balance and alignment. A great goal is one hour of massage each week. A minimum goal is one hour of massage a month. An ounce of prevention is worth a pound of cure.

Massage also allows you to disconnect with the "busyness" of life. There's a lot to be said for that. Simply put, I believe folks who get regular massages are just happier human beings.

Chiropractic and Physical Therapy. Alert. Alert. Alert. You do NOT need to be hurt to see a chiropractor. As a matter of fact, I'm going to encourage you to visit a skilled chiropractor BEFORE you get hurt. Chiropractors can really help your neuromuscular system as well as your skeletal system. They do far more than adjust the spine.

Nowadays, many chiropractors infuse highly touted, progressive protocols as part of their treatment services: ART (active release technique), cold-laser therapy, Graston, kinesiology taping, and much more.

Chiropractors and physical therapists can play a pivotal role in helping you perform and feel your best. Their services should not only be associated with recovery from injury.

Foam Rolling. Some call it "poor man's massage." I say it's a "smart ADDITION to massage." Foam rolling creates self myo-fascial release (myo = muscle; fascia = connective tissue enveloped around every tendon, ligament, nerve, muscle, bone, and organ of the body). You can do this practically anyplace, anywhere. Purchase an inexpensive foam roller or Grid for less than $40, and use it EVERY DAY. Just 10 to 15 minutes on the mid-thoracic region, glutes, IT-band, calves, quads, and lats will go a long way toward soft tissue pliability. This is a GREAT thing.

One of my original coaches/mentors, Tom House, taught me something so important when he said, "You are as strong as your weakest link and as efficient as your worst movement." That means if your hips are tight, you can't perform your best. If your back is hurting, you need to find out WHY and do something about it. **LISTEN** to your body and change your routine to address your weaknesses.

You see, I'm convinced that my back injury was the "final straw that broke the camel's back." When I was playing football, I didn't stretch much. I didn't do much yoga. I certainly didn't foam roll or get regular massage and bodywork. I didn't **RECOVER**. I didn't **RESTORE**.

What I did do was a ton of heavy lifting. Power cleans, squats, bench presses. Lots of reps. Lots of weight. I did very little core training. Very little rotational training. Very little joint integrity work. Most of my training was uniplanar, despite my position (quarterback) being primarily a multi-planar and rotational activity. I never focused on recovery until I was hurt, and then ALL I THOUGHT OF WAS RECOVERY. **Where was the yin to my world of yang?**

Today, I wonder what *could have been* had I done things differently back then. I will never know the answer to this, but I know for sure that the experience of injury and recovery made me a much better coach and trainer.

I share this story for one reason: to save you the pain I experienced. Please don't wait and learn this lesson the hard way. Take it from me. Take action TODAY. Restore, recover, and re-energize to start feeling your best.

ACTION STEP

What **"yin"** activities can you add to your current routine to help you perform and feel better? Write them down, commit to them, and most importantly, DO THEM!

See you over at www.ToddDurkin.com/WOWBook-Workouts to make sure you are doing all the right things!

WOW 8
SUSHI GUY—ALL IN?

I've often said that there's nothing worse than being "half in" to something. A job. A relationship. A responsibility. Heck, life for that matter.

People who are "half in" I call fence-walkers. And they do NO good to an organization. They do no good for a business. They do no good for a team. Heck, they do NO good for themselves. Or for you.

Fence-walkers will never find their passion until they commit themselves fully to something and be **ALL IN**.

I met a fence-walker once that just made me shake my head. I had just landed at the John Wayne Airport in Irvine, California, and wanted to catch a bite to eat at a local restaurant. So I opted for sushi and found this little sushi joint in a neighboring strip mall.

As I walked in and sat down, I jokingly said to the waiter, "You guys have the best sushi in Orange County right?"

And he kind of shrugged and didn't say much. That was a red flag to me. So I continued, "Seriously. Do you guys have good sushi?"

Then he replied, "We are OK. But if you want the best in town, it's right down the street."

He SERIOUSLY said that to me.

And then he literally explained where it was at and said that it even was within walking distance.

As quick as you can say, "Jumping Jack LaLanne," I was out of there. And I walked to the "other" sushi place. And he was right—I loved the "other" place.

But that is one employee I would NOT want working for me.

"Oh, yeah, there is a better fitness center down the street. You go out the door, make a right, and you will like it better." Are you kidding me?

Even though I know that would never be the case, I can't believe an employee of a company would actually steer a customer to a "competitor" while the customer was already seated and ready to do business with them.

I left shaking my head. If I were that guy's boss, he would have been fired on the spot.

Hey, I was actually glad he told me about the other place because it was very good. And I had a great meal.

But I couldn't get over the fact of the employee of the first sushi place telling me about the "better" one and essentially prompting me to leave.

Maybe he thought he was being helpful. Maybe he was working the only job he could get. Maybe his parents ran the restaurant, and he was expected to work there—and resented it. I don't know—but his fence walking not only wasn't helping that sushi place—it also wasn't helping him.

Indifferent, lethargic, blasé, uninspired—that's the kind of person he seemed. His head was not in the game.

Hey, sushi guy, we only get this one life, so pick a side and commit. Care more. Love what you do. Live inspired. And no matter what— either be **ALL IN** or be **ALL OUT**. Don't be a fence-walker.

I don't want to play with people on the fence. And neither do you.

What can you do to be more **ALL IN**? And this includes your personal and your professional life. It includes your health and fitness. Your relationships. Your commitment to your learning and your profession. EVERYTHING!

Encourage more. Acknowledge more. Praise more. Be more present. Be more invested. Be a problem-solver, not a problem-seeker. Be the solution and not the problem. And this is for anyone—on a team, in a family, in a relationship, in your pursuit of a new skill or hobby. Be all in.

If you want more, give more. Of anything. Energy, money, leadership, effort, focus, time, presence of mind.

Bottom line . . . If you want more, be **ALL IN**.

And if you don't want in, then get OUT.

Thanks, sushi guy. I appreciate your honesty—but you need to get a new job or get **ALL IN**.

Don't be *THAT* guy or girl.

BE ALL IN!

 **ACTION STEP**

How can you better be **ALL IN** with what you currently do? In your family? In your relationships? At work? In your spiritual life? And with your health, nutrition, and fitness?

Do you need to invest more time, energy, or emotion into being **ALL IN**?

Or do you need to be like the sushi guy and get OUT?

Listen to your gut, make a decision that you believe is best for you, and then be **ALL IN** to what you are doing.

Enjoy your sushi!

WOW 9

CLEANSE

Sometimes you just need to cleanse. To detox. To get the "junk out of the trunk."

It'll make you feel lighter, simpler, and more alive. Refreshed and rejuvenated. Humbled and grateful—to continue doing the difficult but rewarding work of life.

Here are 11 great ways you can **CLEANSE** and **DETOX** your life.

1. **Rise and Shine.** Wake up, stretch, say your morning prayers, and smile. Begin your day with a big glass of water and lemon to help alkalize the body and support elimination.

2. **BE GRATEFUL.** Write in a gratitude journal for ten minutes. Who are you MOST grateful for in your life? What are you MOST grateful for in your life?

3. **BE INSPIRED.** Read or listen to inspirational material for at least ten minutes. It could be a great book you are reading or a podcast in which you listen to something related to business, personal development, or spiritual awakenings.

4. **BE GREEN.** Eat a ton of greens. Or at least have one "green" drink per day.

5. **BE Healthy.** Be sure to eat or drink every three to four hours, so you don't feel hungry and risk an insulin crash.

6. **BE MINDFUL.** Eat your food slowly and savor it.

7. **BE HYDRATED**. Drink a lot of water to help flush toxins and transport nutrients. I always recommend half your body weight in fluid ounces of water.

8. **BE ACTIVE.** Move your body today. Honor it with where you are at. Maybe you need a good sweat. Maybe you need yoga or meditation. Or maybe you need both. And if you are struggling to get it in, do it first thing in the morning. Or hire a coach!

9. **BE PAMPERED.** Rejuvenate every area of your body that needs a little boost. Schedule a massage, facial, or manicure. Or take a warm bath filled with Epsom salts and lavender.

10. **BE RESTED.** Hit the sack early. Aim for at least eight hours of sleep.

11. **DON'T WATCH TV**. TV often contaminates your mindset and fills your time with anything but inspirational material. So avoid it today! (Unless it's NBC STRONG of course :))

CLEANSE your body, mind, and spirit today. And every day.

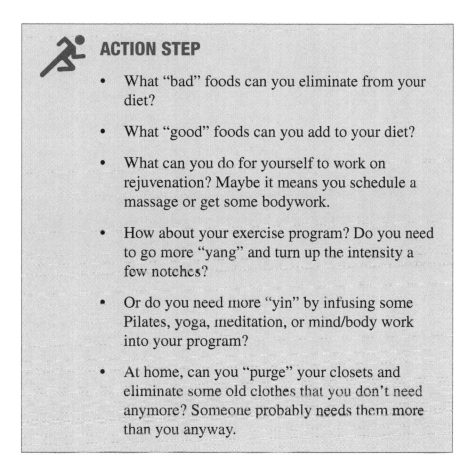

ACTION STEP

- What "bad" foods can you eliminate from your diet?

- What "good" foods can you add to your diet?

- What can you do for yourself to work on rejuvenation? Maybe it means you schedule a massage or get some bodywork.

- How about your exercise program? Do you need to go more "yang" and turn up the intensity a few notches?

- Or do you need more "yin" by infusing some Pilates, yoga, meditation, or mind/body work into your program?

- At home, can you "purge" your closets and eliminate some old clothes that you don't need anymore? Someone probably needs them more than you anyway.

Think about what you can do to further nourish and improve your mind, body, and soul.

And then do it.

WOW 10

BELIEF

If you can believe it . . . you can achieve it.

What I'm about to share is a true story: When Sylvester Stallone wrote his original *Rocky I* script, he was near broke. After countless meetings and tries, no one showed real interest in buying the script.

He was so broke as a starving actor that he could hardly even afford his apartment rent. He was close to living on the streets.

After a couple months, one company finally offered Stallone $30,000 for his script. But the stipulation was that he was not allowed to play Rocky Balboa. And all along, that's what Stallone had wanted. So the company rebuked, and Stallone was told to keep shopping.

Sylvester got so broke that he actually had to sell his dog to pay his rent. And he did. For $50!

And a month later, a different company came by and offered him some money for his script. More importantly, they offered him the role of Rocky Balboa.

And the rest is history.

The six *Rocky* movies went on to gross over $1 billion, and Stallone went on to star in over 60 films. His net worth is now over $400 million.

And it makes me think back to the beginning.

Would you sell your dog because you **believed** in something so much that you knew it was worth something way more than what others put a value on? A script. A product. A program. A business.

That's the **BELIEF** that Stallone had when he had NOTHING. And that's the **BELIEF** it takes when you have EVERYTHING.

Sidenote: In *Rocky I*, the dog Butkus that appears is actually Stallone's real dog that he'd sold. After he got paid, he went back to the person who had bought his dog and Stallone bought Butkus back for $3,000. Now that is awesome! #BELIEF

BELIEF.

It's easy to **believe** when things are going great. It's not easy to **believe** when you are faced with serious adversity, challenge, or obstacles.

I think the Sylvester Stallone example is a great one to depict a real person who has overcome a lot. He had to start somewhere. And where he is today is far different than who he was back before he sold his manuscript. And that's because of his **BELIEF**.

BELIEF . . . It's the thing that often separates winners from losers. It's a lack of **BELIEF** that often stifles people to live in mediocrity their entire lives because they are afraid of the "what ifs."

- *What if . . .* I fail?

- *What if . . .* I succeed?

- *What if . . .* I don't earn a scholarship?

- *What if . . .* I don't get selected for the team?

- *What if . . .* I make money on this program or business, and then lose it all?

- *What if . . .* people make fun of me?

- *What if* . . . people ridicule me or hate me or don't like me?

- *What if* . . . I'm ahead of my time with this idea, and it doesn't work out?

- *What if* . . . someone is already doing something similar to what I'm doing?

- *What if* . . . I lose my job?

- *What if* . . . I don't have benefits?

- *What if* . . . ?

- *What if* . . . ?

- *What if* . . . ?

- *What if* . . . you stopped saying WHAT IF?

And start saying, WHEN I . . .

- *When I* . . . fail, I will get back up and do it over again, and be smarter and better.

- *When I* . . . succeed, I'm going to be able to have more time, freedom, and money freedom, and I'll help give back to society even more.

- *When I* . . . fail and people make fun of me, I will use it as fuel to continue building my life.

- *When I* . . . TRY, I will be content to know that I did my best and that I will continue to move forward each and every day.

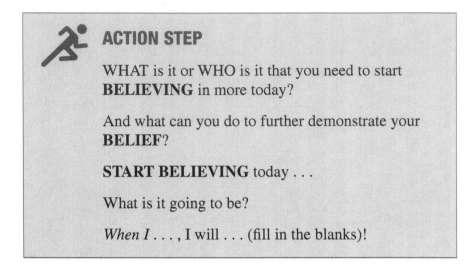

ACTION STEP

WHAT is it or WHO is it that you need to start **BELIEVING** in more today?

And what can you do to further demonstrate your **BELIEF**?

START BELIEVING today . . .

What is it going to be?

When I . . . , I will . . . (fill in the blanks)!

And then, ultimately, you must **BELIEVE IT!**

There is an additional article on BELIEF on the WOW website: www.ToddDurkin.com/WOWbook-Belief.

WOW 11
LOVE

One of the best coaches of all time is Coach John Wooden. He won an unprecedented ten national championships at UCLA from 1964 to 1975.

He amassed 664 wins and only 162 losses (an over 80% win percentage).

He is the first person to be inducted to the Basketball Hall of Fame as both a player and a coach (he was a three-time All American at Purdue).

And the list goes on and on . . .

Coach Wooden was also an author. And one of my favorite books of all time is his *Pyramid of Success*. In the book, he shares his twenty-one principles of success.

And Coach Wooden talks about how hard work and enthusiasm are the cornerstones of success.

Fast-forward many years after he first published his book. It was actually after one of the last talks he gave before he died at the age of 99.

A reporter asked, "Coach Wooden, a question on your *Pyramid of Success* book. Thirty years after you wrote that book, if you were to write another edition, would you change anything about the book? Would you add anything or take anything out of the pyramid?"

Coach Wooden thought for a moment and then replied, "I wouldn't change any of the words because all of the words are still great principles to success.

"But I did leave one word out. And that word should be smack in the middle of my pyramid.

"And that word is **LOVE**.

"For I would never would have won ten national championships without **LOVING** my players. I could not have helped mold my players as men without **LOVING** them. Yes, **LOVE**. **LOVE** should be smack in the middle of my pyramid."

Now that is powerful.

One of the best gifts I have ever received was an autographed copy of Coach Wooden's *Pyramid of Success*. On it, he wrote these words:

"Success is a peace of mind which is a direct result of self-satisfaction in knowing you did your best to become the best that you are capable of becoming."

Now those are some wise words from the "Wizard of Westwood."

ACTION STEP

How can you **LOVE** more this week?

Who can you spend more time with?

How can you express your appreciation for them more?

What can you do to let them know that you truly and genuinely care for them?

Thanks for the great lesson, Coach Wooden. Time to make sure that **LOVE** is in the center of all we do.

Much **LOVE** . . . and much SUCCESS!

WOW 12
BREAKTHROUGH

 They say that big-time players step up in big-time games. And I think most players dream of having **breakout** performances.

I was sitting inside the RCA Dome in Indianapolis, Indiana, in 2012, watching a crop of NFL Combine athletes, each doing his best to have a **BREAKOUT** performance.

Yes, each and every one of the three hundred-plus invited athletes in attendance all have had massive success thus far in their athletic careers to put them in the position to succeed.

Great high school careers.

College scholarships.

All-Star and All-American statuses in college.

Records broken.

But more importantly, there was a lot of hard work. There was a lot of sweat, blood, tears, and adversity that many times went unnoticed. And of course, there were a lot of dreams.

And these athletes were there at that one moment in time searching for that one **BREAKOUT** performance. Something that would separate them from everyone else in the greatest job interview of their life.

A blazing forty-yard dash, an incredible bench press, outstanding field work, and solid interviews are all part of the process of ultimately providing these young men the opportunity of a lifetime. Realized dreams. Potential reached. Financial freedom. The knowingness that you gave it your all and succeeded.

Aren't we like these NFL Combine athletes in many ways? Constantly searching for a **BREAKOUT** performance.

Unfortunately, sometimes there are breakdowns before there are breakouts or breakthroughs. **Breakdowns** often lead to **breakthroughs**. **Breakthroughs** allow us to have **breakouts**!

Sometimes, it takes years and years and years of hard work and toil to "get it right."

Sometimes our course will get redirected several times until our exact purpose is aligned perfectly with our passion.

But the bottom line is this: As we continue to work hard for our own **BREAKTHROUGHS** and **breakouts**, know that it is the cumulative effect of our daily actions and discipline that sets you up for excellence. Dreams, passion, surrounding yourself with people that elevate your mindset, hard work, and the ability to focus on "winning" each and every day. That's what builds greatness. That's what builds champions.

Whether you want a **BREAKTHROUGH** in your business and professional world or a **BREAKTHROUGH** in your personal world, focus your mind on the discipline and determination it takes to do the little things that will ultimately lead to your **BREAKTHROUGH**.

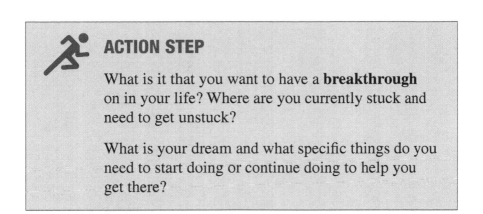

ACTION STEP

What is it that you want to have a **breakthrough** on in your life? Where are you currently stuck and need to get unstuck?

What is your dream and what specific things do you need to start doing or continue doing to help you get there?

Define it. Write it down. Read it over and over again. Work at it. Practice it. Continue to hone your craft. And do all the necessary things needed to have your **breakthrough**!

WOW 13

RITUALS

My kids used to swim competitively. And while they competed for different reasons, they both spent a lot of time working on swimming.

While my son Luke (ten at the time) swam like a fish and was very competitive, my eight-year-old son Brady was quite the opposite. While Luke loved to compete, Brady did not love the meets so much.

As a matter of fact, something happened at his first meet that proved to be a big life lesson . . .

On the day of his first meet, Brady woke up feeling "sick."

I explained it was just butterflies and nerves in his stomach. He had a tough time comprehending that and insisted he was sick. Melanie and I were quite confident it was just a bad case of the jitters.

So we made him go to the meet.

Let me preface this by saying swim meets are long. Really long. Your child swims for about a minute and then has two hours off before the next race. Did I say these meets are long? Yeah.

And let's just say that I don't necessarily love sitting around all day waiting for a 30-second race. And it's even worse when your son is moaning that he can't swim, that he's scared, and that he's not sure he can do it.

I tried every mental trick of the trade—breathing techniques, visualization/imagery exercises, getting him in the warm-up pool, positive talk/mantras—you name it, I tried it.

Bottom line was that he just needed to get in the darned pool and compete. But he wasn't going to race until about noon. And it was still only 10 am. Ugghhhh!!!

About twenty minutes before his race, Brady really started to get worked up and scared. I talked to Coach Shawn and told him how Brady was feeling, that Brady was just nervous as heck. You know how sometimes your own kids listen to their coaches more than you? Yeah, even my kids are the same way!

As a matter of fact, I was about to just pick him up, throw him in the pool, and chase him if he didn't turn it around quickly. Miraculously, Brady mustered up the courage, jumped in, and competed in the 50-meter freestyle.

He came in last place—and I was so dang proud.

He shot out so fast in the race that he was actually first for the initial 25 meters. And then he just fizzled.

And it didn't even matter. He competed. And he did his best.

He immediately felt better after the race, and it proved to him that it was just nerves.

Lesson learned—COMPETE.

Now let me share with you the cornerstone behind the COMPETE lesson. The cornerstone is **RITUAL**.

Every night, we have a bedtime **RITUAL** in our family. This is what Luke, Brady, and McKenna say to Melanie and me:

I'm so happy, I can do anything, and I love my mom and dad.

Melanie and I then say back:

I'm so happy, I can do anything, and I love Luke, Brady, and McKenna.

And then altogether, we say:

We're the Durkins . . . We always do OUR BEST, and WE NEVER GIVE UP.

Something I pointed out to Brady on the way home from the meet that day was that his swim was a great example of "doing your best" and "never giving up."

It's one thing to say it; it's another to do it. And it's when you're scared, it's when you have anxiety, it's when you have FEAR, that you have to remember what you most deeply stand for and believe in.

But by practicing a **RITUAL**, saying it every night, it gets in your head that you must LIVE by it.

Lesson reinforced. **RITUALS** count!

And practicing a **RITUAL** that gives you the strength of heart and mind to jump in and start kicking when the time comes will only ensure that you live out your best self.

 **ACTION STEP**

Identify where in your life—work, family, friends, fitness, etc.—you feel some fear.

What **RITUALS** and routines can you develop to help you be more confident in this area that might be scaring the heck out of you?

Now start practicing those **RITUALS** and routines, every single day, so you can dive in and ATTACK head-on! Be a contender! Live out your best self!

WOW 14
PEOPLE & LEADERSHIP

I love studying great coaches. In any sport. And on all levels.

One of those coaches is Dick Vermeil. Coach Vermeil coached three different NFL teams. The Philadelphia Eagles. The St. Louis Rams. And the Kansas City Chiefs.

In 1999, he led the Rams to a Super Bowl championship. He amassed 126 wins in his 29-year NFL head-coaching career. And he was a three-time NFL Coach of the Year. He has positively impacted thousands of men in his coaching tenure.

On this one particular evening in 2013, I had the opportunity to hear him speak to a few hundred fitness trainers/pros at a Perform Better conference in Providence, Rhode Island.

And he was awesome!

Coach Vermeil revealed his "Seven Common Sense Coaching Points" that make the foundation for any team, business, company, or family. In all seven points, there was ONE commonality: **PEOPLE**.

Without great **PEOPLE,** there are no great businesses, no great TEAMS, no great organizations, no great families, no great companies, and no great brands.

Coach Vermeil talked about how the most important resource of any company is its **PEOPLE**: their personal dignity, pride in what they do, and the trust that they have in management.

At the end of every business/calendar year an important and first question a **LEADER** should ask is:

Do we have better people in our company?

Do we have better people on December 31st (the year's end), than we did on January first (the year's beginning)?

Are we better TODAY than we were at the start of the year?

Think about what Ford says in its MISSION statement: "Our **PEOPLE** are the source of our strength."

Think about what Hilton Hotels says in its VALUES statement: "**PEOPLE** are our most important asset."

YOU are a **LEADER** of your business, your TEAM, your family, your organization . . . regardless of your title!

Your **PEOPLE** need to know what to expect.
Your **PEOPLE** need to be kept informed.
Your **PEOPLE** need to be trained.
Your **PEOPLE** need to be challenged.
Your **PEOPLE** need to be held accountable.
Your **PEOPLE** need to be appreciated.
Your **PEOPLE** need to feel that you care about them.
Your **PEOPLE** need to be recognized and celebrated.
Your **PEOPLE** need to be **LED**.
Your **PEOPLE** need to be able to grow and advance.
Your **PEOPLE** need your feedback and coaching.
Your **PEOPLE** need to be LISTENED to and HEARD.
Your **PEOPLE** need to be TRUSTED, and they must TRUST YOU!
Your **PEOPLE** must be LOVED and LOVE each other.

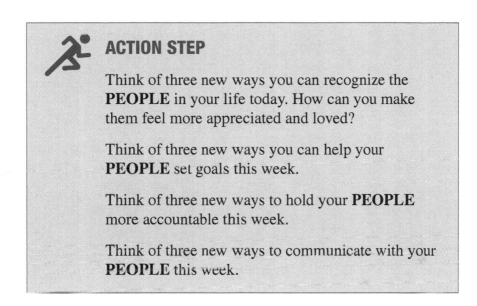

ACTION STEP

Think of three new ways you can recognize the **PEOPLE** in your life today. How can you make them feel more appreciated and loved?

Think of three new ways you can help your **PEOPLE** set goals this week.

Think of three new ways to hold your **PEOPLE** more accountable this week.

Think of three new ways to communicate with your **PEOPLE** this week.

People before PROCESS.

People before PROFITS.

People drive PERFORMANCE.

Celebrate all the **PEOPLE** in your life today. By spending meaningful time with them, building them up, and making them feel appreciated, your day will be more fulfilled, and your **PEOPLE** will be better.

WOW 15
BEST PRACTICES

I was recently asked this question by a client of mine.

"Do you ever go through a period of time (short or long) where you feel stale? And if you do get stale, what is it that gets your juices flowing? What is that one thing you can turn to that revs up your engine? Excites you beyond belief? Pushes you to get better every day?"

Well, to answer the question . . . YES, there are times when I feel stale. And there are times when I feel like I'm on actual fire.

I think that's only human nature to feel both.

But the object is how do we stay more on the "fired-up" side, than the "stale" side, correct?

I believe there are several reasons WHY we sometimes may feel stale. And they typically all deal with our **BEST PRACTICES**. Or lack of doing our **BEST PRACTICES**.

Here are 13 of my **BEST PRACTICES** for you to consider:

1. Get up early.

2. Don't turn your phone on right away in the morning. I wait until my morning routine is done.

3. Prayer time in the morning (or you can call it meditation or quiet time). Minimum ten minutes.

4. Journal time (morning or evening for ten minutes).

5. Eat a great, healthy breakfast . . . and then good foods the rest of the day.

6. Work out daily. Sometimes it's vigorous. Sometimes it's stretching and foam rolling. But do something every day to get better.

7. High-quality sleep (I try to get a minimum of 7 hours).

8. Read or listen to inspirational material that inspires your best thought process. I like listening to podcasts in the morning when doing my cardio work; and while driving, I like listening to recorded talks on business or leadership.

9. Spend time with people that challenge you . . . physically, mentally, emotionally, or spiritually.

10. Get time in nature every week. A hike, a walk at the park, time at the beach or in the mountains, snowshoeing or skiing.

11. Include recovery strategies as part of your weekly plan. Massage, yoga, foam rolling, warm baths in Epsom salts, or hot tubs.

12. Follow a supplementation program to make sure all nutrients, vitamins, and minerals are adequate. I feel this is about 10% of overall nutrition. I advocate at least a multivitamin, fish oils, amino acids, glutamine, and a post-workout recovery drink (2:1 carbs to protein) for most active people.

13. In the 45 minutes before going to bed, don't watch TV. Opt for reading or journaling instead.

If/when you do these things, you typically are going to feel fired up and ready to conquer the world.

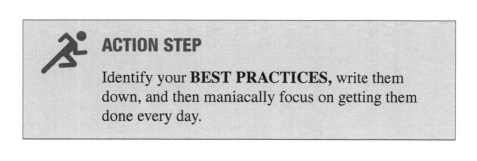

ACTION STEP

Identify your **BEST PRACTICES,** write them down, and then maniacally focus on getting them done every day.

WOW 16
BARRIERS & BRIDGES

On June 5, 1964, on a clay track in Compton, California, America's Jim Ryun became the first high school runner to break four minutes for the mile, running 3:59.0 as a junior hailing from Wichita East High School in Wichita, Kansas.

Then as a senior, he beat his own time again when he ran a 3:55.3. That record stood for thirty-six years.

Think about that. Running under a four-minute mile. That's crazy. Even when you were in the BEST shape of your life, could you run around a track in under sixty seconds? And then repeat it three more times?

I think I was in the best shape of my life when I was in my early 20s and playing college football. And at that point, I could get around a track in one minute and sixteen seconds. ONE TIME. Not four times. Ugghhh.

Only five high schoolers have EVER run under four minutes in a mile. That's four times around a track. Interesting to think that three people did this in the late 1960s. After Ryun, Tim Danielson broke the barrier in 1966, and Marty Liquori ran a sub-four-minute mile in 1967.

And it wasn't until Alan Webb ran 3:53.43 in 2001 that Ryun's record fell. And then in 2011, Lukas Verzbicas became the fifth high schooler to run a mile under four minutes.

Kind of interesting that Ryun broke the record and then two other people did that in subsequent years. And then nothing until 2001. That's thirty-six years without any single high schooler running under a four-minute mile.

Could it have been that the switch to the metric system in track and field in the 1970s meant fewer races at the mile distance?

Could it have been that the trend in the 1980s and '90s, in large part, was for young track athletes to undergo less intense training sessions?

Could it be that these guys in the late 1960s were just that good?

Bottom line is this—only five high schoolers have EVER accomplished this feat. And that is quite amazing.

(Remember, Roger Bannister actually broke the four-minute mile in 1954, but he was a graduate medical student, not a high schooler—big difference).

Our WOW is **BARRIER and BRIDGES**.

Until Ryun ran a sub-four-minute mile, there was major speculation whether a high school runner could accomplish this. It stood as a **BARRIER**.

And then once Ryun did it, he ripped the lid off the **BARRIER**, and it served as a **BRIDGE** to prove that it could be done.

Why is **BARRIER** part of our WOW?

Because you have to face **BARRIERS** in your life. Every day. And you must embrace them. Tackle them. Hurdle them.

Is it your mindset?

Your belief system?

Is it your environment?

Is it your current job situation?

So when does a **BARRIER** (whether it be a sub-four-minute mile or throwing 5,000 passing yards in a season) become a **BRIDGE** to inspire **GREATNESS** and breakthrough achievements?

Jim Ryun broke a **BARRIER**, thus making a **BRIDGE** so that two other high schoolers (Liquori and Danielson) followed with similar breakthroughs in subsequent years.

Dan Marino had the single season 5,000+ yards passing record since 1984. Then Drew Brees, Tom Brady, and Peyton Manning subsequently broke through this feat in 2012, 2013, and 2014, respectively.

Why and how did the **BARRIER** become a **BRIDGE** to greatness?

There are many other examples in SPORTS and in LIFE when a seemingly insurmountable challenge/obstacle (**BARRIER**) is broken and then leads to similar achievement by others (**BRIDGE**).

What determines whether a **BARRIER** will be broken?

Training? Talent? Mindset? Hard work? Focus? Inspiration or motivation from another? Great coaching? Desire? Self-preservation (in certain cases of survival)?

Think about your business—what is it that you WANT to DO, but for whatever reason, you have not been able to create a breakthrough to "get it done"? Is it talent, tools, time, fear, or lack of motivation or inspiration that is acting as a **BARRIER**?

That is where others come in. Maybe it is a Jim Ryun or a Jackie Robinson or a Neil Armstrong taking that first step on the Moon ("One small step for man, one giant leap for mankind"), who showed the courage and fortitude to perform and break through **BARRIERS**, experience GREATNESS, and create the **BRIDGE** to open it up and INSPIRE others to do the same.

> **ACTION STEP**
>
> Examine your life or business and identify what **BARRIERS** you need to overcome. Write down your current **BARRIERS**.
>
> Furthermore, write down what can happen to your life and business once you build the **BRIDGE** to remove those **BARRIERS**.

A **BARRIER** is a **BRIDGE**. Without **BARRIERS**, there are no **BRIDGES** to higher achievement.

A **BARRIER** is NOT to be perceived as a red light to the way things are, but rather a green light as to the way things can be!

Attack your **BARRIERS**. Create your **BRIDGES**. And have massive breakthroughs!

WOW 17
VORACIOUS

I need to share an amazing feat with you. Like really amazing.

And it deals with my son Brady when he was just eight years old.

In September 2013, my wife, Melanie, gave Brady his first *Harry Potter* book—*Harry Potter and the Sorcerer's Stone*. He fell in love with the book, devouring it in less than four weeks. The book is 309 pages. Fairly impressive for a young kid.

And before you know it, the kid started devouring every *Harry Potter* book. Nonstop. Absolutely **VORACIOUS**.

And six months later, by March 2014, Brady finished his last *Harry Potter* book. And there were seven books overall.

Here are the books, how long they are, and how long each took Brady to devour:

Book 2: *Harry Potter and the Chamber of Secrets* (341 pages)— 2 weeks

Book 3: *Harry Potter and the Prisoner of Azkaban* (421 pages)— 1 week

Book 4: *Harry Potter and the Goblet of Fire* (724 pages)—6 weeks

Book 5: *Harry Potter and the Order of the Phoenix* (870 pages)— 8 weeks

Book 6: *Harry Potter and the Half-Blood Prince* (652 pages)—
4 weeks

Book 7: *Harry Potter and the Deathly Hallows* (759 pages)—
5 weeks

What's even more amazing is Brady just recited these titles to me, the number of pages in each of them, and how long it took him to complete each book—*without even looking at them.*

Brady is a **VORACIOUS** reader. Here, he read 4,076 pages in six months at the age of eight. And he can tell you the name of every chapter in every book from the seven books. I'm not sure where he gets that from because even though I read a ton, I can't tell you the name of the chapter I read just last night!

VORACIOUS. It is defined as "exceedingly eager or avid; having an insatiable appetite for an activity or pursuit."

A **VORACIOUS** reader. A **VORACIOUS** collector. A **VORACIOUS** gardener. A **VORACIOUS** learner of American history. A **VORACIOUS** guitar player.

How about you? What are you **VORACIOUS** about? What do you love to do so much that you just can't put it down, you can't stop?

What can you wrap your arms around so much that you just can't get enough of?

Identify what you love to do and make sure you do more of it. Maybe it's just today. Or just this week or month. Or for the next six months. Perhaps even longer.

But be **VORACIOUS**. Be fully immersed in an activity that you **LOVE** to do and that's good for your mind, body, and/or spirit.

Now go do it!

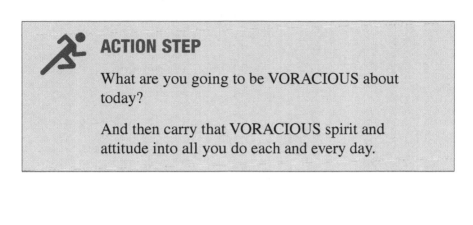

ACTION STEP

What are you going to be VORACIOUS about today?

And then carry that VORACIOUS spirit and attitude into all you do each and every day.

WOW 18

JERSEY STRONG

On October 29, 2012, Hurricane Sandy ravaged the entire Eastern Seaboard. And it devastated the Jersey Shore and the place I grew up, Brick, New Jersey.

Friends and family lost everything.

My sister Judy lost her home.

My sister Patti was displaced from her business for months.

All in all, over 650,000 people lost homes or were displaced.

The hurricane was estimated to cost $75 billion in total damage.

I remember when I saw the initial footage of Point Pleasant, Bay Head, Mantoloking, and Seaside, where the eye of the storm hit, right in the heart of the home community where I grew up.

My heart sank. I felt so helpless being 3,000 miles away in San Diego.

Forty-eight hours passed before I actually talked to three of my sisters who lived there because of downed wires, interrupted cell service, and the chaos that followed.

I knew it was bad. Real bad.

My sisters Patti, Mary Beth, and Judy painted a bleak picture of what they had heard and seen. They said it was horrific there. Literally like a war zone.

When I finally saw a twenty-six-minute aerial video via a helicopter of the entire shore depicting the areas that were most IMPACTED, I just wept. It was devastated. It was wiped out. Lives were lost or impacted forever. I felt the pain that so many people were feeling.

And then I thought about the people. Jersey people. They're different (in a good way!). They really are. People from New Jersey are damned strong. Extremely strong-willed with a tremendous sense of spirit. Great PRIDE. Hardworking. Go-getters. In New Jersey, it is called **JERSEY STRONG**.

And that is an ATTITUDE, an attitude of perseverance. One that is predicated to overcome adversity.

This attitude could best be summed up by one of my best friends growing up, Bill Kleissler. Bill and I grew up together in Brick. We played Pop Warner football together. And then high school football together. And we have always remained close. Always will. Bill is now the principal at Brick Township High School.

Bill shared, "Todd, you don't understand the number of people helping out. It truly is amazing. Not ONE person is hanging their head and moping around. There is a tremendous SPIRIT going on, and people are just doing whatever it takes. The Brick alumni, current Brick football team, and countless volunteers are literally going from house to house in Brick and surrounding areas to clean them out.

"We are pulling out carpet, debris, couches, furniture, and anything left in the destruction. We are serving food with FEMA at the Brick Little League field. We are . . ."

Bill didn't need to say anything else.

JERSEY STRONG.

Tens of thousands of people volunteered their time during that ordeal to help out their brothers and sisters in a very difficult period. And that happened in New Jersey, New York, Long Island, Staten Island, and up and down the Eastern Seaboard.

Hey, we are all going to weather major "storms" in our life. There is tragedy. There are natural disasters. Disease. And sometimes life shortchanges you of what you desire or wish.

As my pastor Miles McPherson once said, "If you are feeling sorry for yourself, just go out and find someone that has it worse off than you. Because there is ALWAYS someone that has it worse than you."

In the tough times, clamor together and serve one another. And remember, it's always about the ATTITUDE you bring to any calamity that counts. Hang strong. **Jersey Strong**—wherever you LIVE!

 **ACTION STEP**

Where do you need to be **Jersey Strong** in your life? What is most challenging you today? What "hurricanes" are going on in your life that you need to get through by being extremely strong?

Now dig down deep, surround yourself with positive people that understand your fight, and remember to always serve others going through difficult times. #JerseyStrong

WOW 19
SIMPLIFY

 I LOVE **progress**. I LOVE **forward motion**. And I LOVE what I call "**moving the needle**."

"**Moving the needle**" means doing those pertinent things in your life you need to do NOW, so you can accomplish what you want to accomplish later.

When you think about the term "**moving the needle**," it takes a lot of FOCUS.

And when you are focused, doing work that resonates with your soul and living in alignment in all aspects of life, life is often **SIMPLER**. Not easier, but **SIMPLER**.

Think about that—**SIMPLIFY**.

How can you **SIMPLIFY** your life? Your business?

Let's look at a few examples of **SIMPLICITY** in action.

Some might say that Washington and Lincoln were **SIMPLE** leaders. But they sure were great leaders. They knew what was really important:

- Lead by example.

- Respect all people.

- Show courage.

- Align with a strong purpose.

- Overcome adversity.

My highly successful high school football coach practiced **SIMPLICITY**. Coach Wolf demanded execution of just a few plays instead of having a playbook of dozens of plays that weren't mastered. He was famous for saying, "Run it again," over and over until the same play was perfected. And that led to massive success. (You can read more about Coach Wolf in WOW 2 LABOR.)

Legendary NFL Green Back Packers and Hall of Fame football coach Vince Lombardi's "sweep right" and "sweep left" were **SIMPLE** and executed precisely. And it led to many championships.

John Wooden's full-court press was **SIMPLE** in many ways. But it caused mass confusion for UCLA's opponents. And it is one thing that helped UCLA earn ten NCAA basketball championships. (You can read more about Coach Wooden in WOW 11 LOVE)

Often, the greatest coaches demand executing the **SIMPLEST** strategies. They don't confuse their athletes. The athletes must master the fundamentals and perfect them. And then play to their strengths.

How about **SIMPLICITY** in the business aspect?

SIMPLICITY says "less is more." **SIMPLICITY** often allows your TEAM to have a sense that there are specific practices and systems that are basic to being successful. A team can gain confidence because of consistency of purpose and familiarity of a method, approach, or culture.

Perfect the **SIMPLICITY**—eliminate the unnecessary.

Two great examples in the business world of mastering **SIMPLICITY** are Starbucks and Apple.

Starbucks is maniacally focused on ONE CUP . . . ONE CUSTOMER . . . ONE EXPERIENCE. And they are wildly successful.

And APPLE. Think about how "SIMPLE" an Apple product is. But think about how "complex" it is. The user experience is **SIMPLE**, easy to navigate, and a seven-year-old can figure out how to use it. But behind the simplicity lies an empire that is so robust and powerful.

Ralph Waldo Emerson stated, "To be **SIMPLE** is to be great."

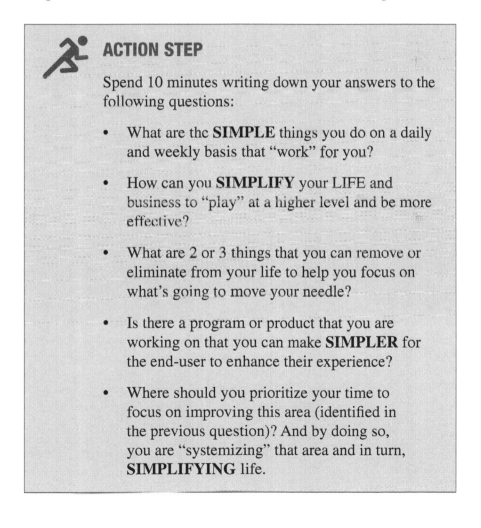

ACTION STEP

Spend 10 minutes writing down your answers to the following questions:

- What are the **SIMPLE** things you do on a daily and weekly basis that "work" for you?

- How can you **SIMPLIFY** your LIFE and business to "play" at a higher level and be more effective?

- What are 2 or 3 things that you can remove or eliminate from your life to help you focus on what's going to move your needle?

- Is there a program or product that you are working on that you can make **SIMPLER** for the end-user to enhance their experience?

- Where should you prioritize your time to focus on improving this area (identified in the previous question)? And by doing so, you are "systemizing" that area and in turn, **SIMPLIFYING** life.

SIMPLIFY your life today and be maniacally focused on what is most going to help you **move your needle**.

Be SIMPLE and Be GREAT!

WOW 20

WRITE

Writing creates clarity . . . and clarity precedes genius.
—Robin Sharma, Writer and Speaker

It baffles me how many kids can't **WRITE** well these days. I'm not sure if it's because of the "texting" age we live in or the lack of focus on writing skills in our schools, but I'm always saddened when I see poor writing.

On the other hand, it excites me when I read a great book or a great application or even an email.

For me, I learned to **WRITE** well in the seventh grade. I was nominated to be a Pop-Warner Scholar-Athlete. Only thirty-five middle school kids in all of the US would be selected, and it was based on scholastic achievement, athletic accomplishment in Pop Warner, and the seven essays each kid had to write.

That task was daunting to me. I wasn't much of a writer then.

But my dad took me down to the basement where our Ping-Pong table was, laid out all the questions, and began to teach me how to **WRITE** on those big, yellow legal notepads.

He had me "flow with the pen." (Remember, there were not computers in 1984. It was all handwritten. OMG, I'm dating myself ☺.)

He had me **WRITE** stories. He told me to keep my pen flowing and not to stop and think. And he would time me for five minutes and see how much I could get down on paper in that time.

He told me you always have to have a great, eye-catching opener. And a strong finisher.

And he told me to **WRITE** with emotion and soul.

Maybe you don't love to **WRITE**. Or maybe you never have worked at it. It's kind of like exercise or sport. If you want to be good at it, you must work at it.

And when you do, it can be transformational.

Your WOW is to **WRITE**.

Why is **WRITE** your WOW? Because writing is critical for success.

As of the writing of this very WOW, I have two "big" writing-related things I'm working on:

1. This very book that you now hold in your hands. If it weren't a priority, it would have never gotten done. And you wouldn't be reading it. ☺

2. My annual roadmap and strategic plan. I do this at the beginning of every year and spend between 10 and 20 hours on fifty-plus questions that I have created to help me craft my most amazing year. I review it periodically throughout the year as well to make sure I'm on track.

And on a daily, weekly, and/or regular basis, I **WRITE** (or type) the following:

1. My "WLAGs" each Sunday night.

   ➢ *Wins*. Wins from the past week.

   ➢ *Losses*. Losses from the past week.

   ➢ *Ahas*. What were the "aha" moments from the past week.

   ➢ *Goals*. What are my top goals for the upcoming week.

(You can see a sample on the WOW website at www.ToddDurkin.com/WOWBook-Write.)

2. My "3 in 30."

What 3 goals will I accomplish in the next 30 days on my "10 Forms of Wealth" wheel? I do this writing once per month.

 (See the WOW website for all details at www.ToddDurkin.com/WOWBook-Write.)

3. My "90-Day Wonder."

Ask yourself these 3 questions and do the exercise every 90 days.

1. What have I accomplished in the past 90 days?

2. What are my present challenges, obstacles, and issues?

3. What WILL I accomplish in the next 90 days?

 See the WOW website for a sample "90-Day Wonder" at www.ToddDurkin.com/WOWBook-Write.)

4. Gratitude journal. I do this several times per week. (See WOW 44 GRATITUDE to learn more about the gratitude journal.)

Writing takes planning and commitment to sit your booty down and actually **WRITE**. But you just have to DO IT.

And that's what I'm going to encourage YOU to do this week—
WRITE.

Here are some things you can potentially **WRITE** about:

- Write an article for your blog or newsletter.

- Write a love letter.

- Write a thank-you note.

- Write in your journal.

- Write a business plan.

- Write a handwritten note to a teammate.

- Write out your Big 5 for the week (what 5 things MUST you accomplish this week to make it a winning week?).

- Write a new workout plan.

- Write your spouse, significant other, or partner a love note.

- Write the first chapter of your book.

- Write your next presentation.

- Write a kick-a** newsletter.

- Write your eulogy (what would others say about you?).

- Write a tweet or write ten tweets for the upcoming week.

- Write a Facebook post or schedule seven of them.

- Write about what you love in life.

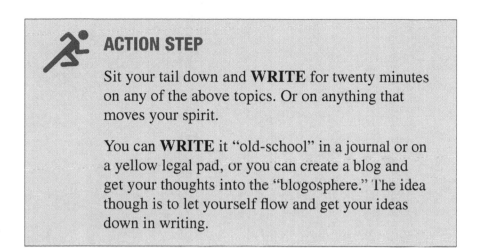

ACTION STEP

Sit your tail down and **WRITE** for twenty minutes on any of the above topics. Or on anything that moves your spirit.

You can **WRITE** it "old-school" in a journal or on a yellow legal pad, or you can create a blog and get your thoughts into the "blogosphere." The idea though is to let yourself flow and get your ideas down in writing.

Commit to **WRITING** this week and watch how it transforms your life.

I say it all the time: "If you want to be an expert and expand your brand, **WRITE** more and SPEAK more."

If you want to unleash your spirit and soul, **WRITE** more.

I hope you realize that with consistent practice, writing will become easier and almost cathartic.

And when it does, **WRITE** me a letter and thank me. I'm just paying forward what my dad taught me!

So get after it. START WRITING!

WOW 21
"LT"

LaDainian Tomlinson was one of the best running backs to ever play in the NFL. And I had the great fortune of training him for most of his career. He actually wrote the foreword to my first book, *The IMPACT Body Plan*, along with his long-time training partner, Drew Brees.

Fitness professionals and young kids often ask me the same questions:

How did you first start working with professional athletes?

Who was your first pro athlete?

Who are some of your favorite pro athletes you've ever worked with and why?

Three questions. One answer: *LaDainian Tomlinson.*

I first met LaDainian when I was a sports massage therapist with the San Diego Chargers back in 2002. He came up to me at the end of the season and said, "I understand you do some 'different' type of training. Some 'functional training.' I'd like to call you when the season is over."

It was January 2003. And the phone rang. A Monday morning and the Chargers season had just ended the day before.

It was LaDainian Tomlinson, and he said he wanted to start training ASAP. He said he was hungry to get started. He told me he wanted "to be one of the best ever to play the game." He told me he was willing to do whatever it took to live up to his heroes: Walter Payton, Emmitt Smith, and Barry Sanders.

We scheduled a session for the next day.

Man, I remember being so nervous before that session. He was the big-star running back in town. He was adored by ALL San Diego fans. He was often hailed as "the future savior of Charger football" and "the one who would return them back to the promised land."

I don't think I slept that night. I was still a young trainer, just shy of thirty-two years old. I was always an athlete myself and worked with a lot of athletes. But I had never trained someone of quite the same stature as LaDainian Tomlinson. I remember driving over early that morning for our 8 am session and feeling sick to my stomach. I really thought I was going to puke. I was so nervous.

Everything changed when he walked into Fitness Quest 10. For those of you who have ever seen LT smile, you know he has a million-dollar smile. He looked so happy to be there and was over-the-top friendly and grateful.

My tension eased, but I was still nervous as heck on the inside.

At the time, Fitness Quest 10 was just about 2,000 square feet. Nothing fancy. Nothing elaborate. Just a lot of passion and energy. And I was really excited. This was like a dream come true for me. I founded my company to work with ALL people under one roof—athletes, kids, older adults, overweight people, out-of-shape folks, and people who are injured. This January day in 2003 marked a special day in history.

The Test

One of the first things I did with LaDainian after warming him up was a one-legged balance touch test. Sixty seconds on the right.

Sixty seconds on the left. Compare the sides and see what comes about.

LaDainian's results: thirty-two touches on one side. Twenty-three on the other. And on the weaker side, he was bouncing around on one leg like a flamingo. A light bulb went off.

As I pointed out the imbalances in his hips and with his balance, it all of the sudden just clicked.

And for nine straight years, we forged a relationship that was truly special.

Here are 21 memories, traits, and stories I love to share about working with #21 for over 9 years.

1. **Hard work.** It has to be #1. There are hard workers, and then there are hard workers. I don't know if I will ever have the chance to work with anyone quite like LT again. He never missed a session. I don't really know if he was even late for a session. And when he was training, the pace was furious. It is no mistake why he was great. Hard work!

2. **"Play like a scared rabbit."** I remember once asking LT what he thought about when he was running the ball. He responded, "I like to play like a scared rabbit. Have you ever seen a scared rabbit get caught? That's the way I like to play."

3. **LT was a throwback.** Walter Payton, Emmitt Smith, and Barry Sanders were his guys. He emulated them. He watched tape on them. He wanted to train like them. Heck, he even built a hill in his backyard to train on just like the legendary hill Walter Payton used to run on. LT had the heart of a lion, the work ethic of a mule, the body of a thoroughbred, and the humility of a young boy still working to make the varsity team.

4. **The *Rocky IV* soundtrack.** For years and years, we listened to that music. Something about hanging off the rafters, pushing past barriers, and the desire to be a champion—that music epitomizes LaDainian Tomlinson. And every time it's played in the gym now, I can't help but think of #21.

5. **Always trying to learn.** Whether it was training or in bodywork, he always wanted to know *how* it was going to help him. And if it made sense to him, he would never question WHY we were doing something. EVER.

6. **Trust.** LT and I built a unique relationship. In the foreword to my *IMPACT* book, he likened our relationship to that of a boxer and his trainer. To me, it was more like that of a "prize-fighter." LaDainian trusted my judgment and programming. More importantly, he trusted me as a human being.

7. **NFL Walter Payton Man of the Year.** In 2006, LaDainian earned the NFL's Man of the Year. This is voted upon for "off the field" work as much as on-the-field contribution. That year, LT won the award and his training partner of three years at the time, Drew Brees, was his co-recipient. Of all accolades, I know the Man of the Year meant the world to LaDainian.

8. **LT Magic.** 2006. It truly was a magical year. The year LT broke the NFL record for all-time touchdowns in a season (31). The year he won the NFL League MVP. I remember being at the stadium that late December day, and the crowd was chanting "LT, LT, LT . . . MVP . . . MVP . . . MVP." I remember thinking to myself, "If only I could just bottle this up and capture it forever." It seemed like all his hard work had paid off, and he was at the prime of his career. I remember getting watery-eyed listening to the crowd chant. In some ways, I felt like a proud father. In some ways, I felt like his trainer. And in some ways, I just felt like every

other one of the 70,000 fans in attendance appreciating the moment. What a memory.

9. **Whatever it takes—WIT.** I have already talked about LT's work ethic. He did NOT miss training days. In the prime of his career, he had a lot of commercials, appearances, interviews, and commitments. Training came first. If that meant he had to train at 5:30 am or 6:00 am, he would do it. WIT—Whatever it takes.

10. **The Headband.** Man, so often he would wear that old-school headband when he worked out. And watch out when he did. That meant he was going into turbo-mode wearing that headband. There was something special about seeing him with that thing.

11. **Very few really liked working out with LT.** It's because they couldn't hang. He trained at an extreme high-intensity pace. There were only a few who consistently trained with him over the nine years I trained LT that could actually hang—Brees, Justin Peelle, Darren Sproles, and a smattering of guys along the way. LaDainian would invite guys in to work out with him. But they would only last about twenty minutes at his pace. And then they would request a different time slot the next time.

12. **A Great LEADER.** He always brought out the best in his workout partners. Having LaDainian and Drew work out together from 2003 to 2009 (that's when LT moved to the Jets) was something else. We had some classic battles. But when either of those two was in a workout, he ALWAYS brought out the best in others.

13. **The day LT buried Reggie Bush.** Man, poor old Reggie was just in college. And Reggie looked up to LaDainian. So LaDainian brought him in for a workout. I remember vividly telling Reggie, "Go slower today than you think you can or

should. You do NOT need to try and keep up with the All-Pro." Well, I knew my words probably weren't going to go far, and they didn't. Reggie was out on the front deck within twenty minutes of training, letting out his breakfast. He hopped back in the workout but instantly knew what he was in for it every time he trained with LT.

14. **15' x 15'.** That is about the size of the sacred space that LT and I trained in about 80% of the time. Core work, balance work, plyos, pushups, pull-ups. We didn't do a lot of weights. We used a lot of bands, cords, medicine balls, dumbbells, and Swiss Balls in the weight room. On the field, we did a lot of agility and speed work. Ladders, cone drills, bungee cord drills for assisted or resisted speed. It was all about trying to make him foundationally strong from feet to fingertips, keep him balanced from left to right, and trying to activate as much fast-twitch fiber as possible. It worked!

15. **"Fridays with LT."** While I trained LT for many years, I also did bodywork/sports massage on him on Friday afternoons before all games. I would do a combination of Rolfing, structural work, soft-tissue work, and stretching. I'd load him up with some arnica and work on his mindset a bit. It was a tradition we had for many years.

16. **The body is a temple.** I reflect back on all that LaDainian did to keep his body in great shape. We trained practically every day in the off-season. Training sessions, speed sessions, and bodywork. He had his own chef. He got acupuncture. He did A.R.T. He did it all. You name it, he probably did it (as long as it was legal). And he always did it the right way. Hard work, dedication, discipline, commitment, and the desire to be the BEST.

17. **Human being.** LT is one of the finest human beings you will ever meet. He cared for people. He would ask about the

people he trained next to. He would ask about the kids who asked for his autograph. He would ask about staff members. He was a bona fide NFL superstar who made everyone feel special. LaDainian is an extremely genuine guy who has taken his blessings and talents as a player and a human being, and made the most of them. He continues to give back and make a positive difference in the community.

18. **Words do mean a lot.** In 2004, I was fortunate to earn Trainer of the Year by IDEA, the world's largest continuing education provider for fitness professionals. In front of a couple thousand people, I was recognized with this distinction. It truly was an award that helped catapult my own career. What made it even more special was that LaDainian had taped a three-minute video message they played in front of everyone, and he said some really amazing things. That memory will last a lifetime.

19. **Family.** I knew him when it was just LT and his wife, LaTorsha. Man, they are like two peas in a pod. She would pull up in her purple Range Rover and would sometimes even train with LaDainian. Let me tell you what—that woman has some genes. Former track and basketball standout. She may even have had faster feet than LT if you can believe it. She loved to box. She loved to compete. Just like her husband.

20. **Why the Jets?** When the writing was on the wall that he was going to be leaving San Diego, he really had two teams he was interested in. Minnesota and New York. The Vikings had Brett Favre and offered more money. The Jets had Rex Ryan. LaDainian chose the Jets. When I asked him why, he told me and his training partners that day, "When I showed up in New York, they had all this Jets baby stuff for my son (Daylen). Baby Jets helmets, baby clothes, etc. It was a done deal. I want my son to see me play someday." The funny thing was that his son was still a few months from being born. That's

the real reason he chose the Jets. Yep. Rex Ryan, you are one smart dude. You went after LaDainian and LaTorsha's soft side, and it worked.

21. **IMPACT.** I am not going to go on about all the records LT has broken and the illustrious career he built. It was not merely a coincidence that all this happened. He worked his butt off, tapped his full potential, and always stayed hungry. He has positively IMPACTED millions of kids and fans through the game of football. And he has always respected what football has provided.

Next stop—Canton!

ACTION STEP

Out of the 21 Traits that made LaDainian great, which one MOST resonates with you? How can you apply this in your life?

LT, thank you. As a coach, a trainer, a proud parent of three kids now myself, and even a fan, I love you, brother. You truly were once-in-a-lifetime. Thanks for everything you have always done.

I'll never forget our first day of training when you told me, "I want to be one of the best to ever play the game."

WOW 22
CHOICES

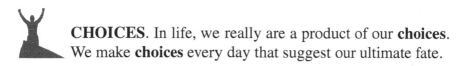 **CHOICES**. In life, we really are a product of our **choices**. We make **choices** every day that suggest our ultimate fate.

I was at dinner with some friends one night, and we were deep in discussion about **choices** in life. With family. Relationships. And even business.

I told them about the time back in 2007 when in the midst of an extremely chaotic 5,000 square foot expansion of Fitness Quest 10, I **CHOSE** to attend a $3,000, three-day workshop by Ali Brown on list-building. Money was a bit tight at the time because of the massive expansion, time was at a premium, and it was at the height of trying to wrap up the expansion and open the new center. The timing just wasn't good for many reasons.

But I **CHOSE** to attend the workshop.

And that workshop was the impetus that changed my on-line business. That was just one **choice** that worked out extremely well.

A while back, Major League Baseball pitcher and client Chris Young spoke at my son Luke's swim banquet. His entire speech to the young boys and girls was on **CHOICES** we make in life. And how every **CHOICE** has a **CONSEQUENCE**. Smoking, drinking, doing your homework, who you hang out with, exercising.

It was an awesome talk by someone who exemplifies a model athlete and citizen. Chris is a Princeton graduate who played over fifteen years in the Big Leagues.

Think about the **choices** you make everyday. Some small. Some big.

How should I spend my off-hour?

Should I spend my money on buying . . . ?

Should I invest my money in . . .?

Should I attend that party?

Should I have a drink or two or three or more tonight?

Should I drive after having "only" two drinks?

Should I text while driving? Or while at a stoplight?

What should I eat for my next meal?

Am I going to work out today?

Do I need to give up the nicotine habit? Or the caffeine habit?

Should I study for that test?

Should I attend that conference?

Should I go to the retreat?

Should I open my business?

Should I get involved in this MLM?

Should I write my book?

How can I best leverage my talents and skills?

Should I hire that person?

Should I fire that person?

Should I write that blog article?

Should I plan out my social media posts for the week?

Should I read that book?

Should I go on that vacation?

How do I best spend my time to maximize my ROI?

Again, some of these **choices** are "small." Some are big. But all of them have consequences. And some of the consequences can lead to great things. And some can lead to extremely detrimental things.

Recently, I was speaking to my kids about this topic of **choices**. We were talking about homework and how every time you do homework, you need to make the **CHOICE** to do it the right way. Slowly. Taking your time. Putting your "signature of approval" on it.

I also talked about how the discipline of doing homework the "right" way over time ultimately allows you to do well in school. And doing well in school allows you to ultimately go to a good college. Or a great one. But it comes down to the **CHOICES** you make every day.

And when making **CHOICES**, you have to listen to both your head AND your gut. Sometimes your head says YES, but your gut says NO. Sometimes your head says NO, but your gut says YES.

I believe it's important to listen to a bit of both your head and your gut when making decisions. I can honestly say that sometimes I listen to my GUT more than my head (Remember WOW 5 GUTS?). I like going by feel and instinct. But that gut always coincides with my finding out the facts also. So it's a bit of a balancing act.

If I would have listened to just my head back in 2007 when attending the workshop on list-building, I would NOT have attended. And I'm so glad I did!

> ### 🏃 ACTION STEP
>
> What **CHOICES** can you make today that will help propel you forward professionally or personally?
>
> Maybe it is **CHOOSING** to DO SOMETHING. Maybe it is **CHOOSING** to eliminate something. Either way, it involves a **CHOICE.**
>
> What do you CHOOSE to do?

Make a **CHOICE**—and then do it.

You never know how "small" **choices** can make such a "BIG" difference.

It's time to **CHOOSE**!

WOW 23
FAIL FORWARD!

Some of the most successful people in the world of all time were failures. Well, I should say—they failed many times. And they continued to get back up each time, dust themselves off, and keep going.

Here are just a few ultra-successful people that sustained major losses or failures along the way:

- Abe Lincoln
- Thomas Edison
- Oprah Winfrey
- Helen Keller
- Michael Jordan
- Steve Jobs
- Arianna Huffington
- Bill Gates
- Jay Z
- Richard Branson
- Walt Disney
- J.K. Rowling
- Stephen King

And the list goes on and on . . .

So how do you overcome failure and get back on the "success train"?

Here are six ways:

1. **You LEARN as much as you possibly can.**

   You continually invest in yourself. In professional development. In personal development. In developing your spiritual self.

   I often say to my Fitness Quest 10 teammates and fellow trainer/coach colleagues, "You can only take a client on a journey as far as you've taken yourself."

   So what are you doing to deepen your personal and professional journey?

2. **You have mantras.**

   Like the mantras I had when I was driving up Pomerado Road when opening Fitness Quest 10 in the year 2000. In the beginning days of my business, I would repeat, "I will not fail . . . I will not fail . . . I will not fail," over and over again while driving into the parking lot.

   While today I would recommend a mantra that is a bit more "positive," my twenty-nine-year-old mindset at the time was still very much in competitive mode.

   Today, my mantra might be "Win the day . . . win the day . . . win the day . . ."

   What are your mantras? What keeps you motivated? What keeps your mind right?

3. **YOU DO IT . . . and DO IT . . . and DO IT!!!**

   As former A.L. Williams and Associates CEO, Art Williams shared in a legendary talk entitled "Just DO IT," you must have the mindset of "DOING IT" regardless of the situation or circumstance. No excuses. Find a way to get the job done and don't stop until you accomplish what you set out to accomplish.

4. You find people that are creating WOW and mimic them.

Imitation is the finest form of flattery. People that are creating WOW are winners. People have a tough time taking their eyes off them.

Find who is performing well in your business or industry, and adhere to their same principles.

5. You remember the "7 Fs."

My good friend and mentor Wayne Cotton taught me many lessons as a young businessman and entrepreneur. One is that "problems create beneficial rearrangements." We are all going to have obstacles, challenges, and issues we are going to face. No one likes problems. But we can all learn from them.

And one of the most powerful things that any human being has ever said to me is when Wayne advised, **"Fear, frustration, and failure are all overcome by faith, focus, forward motion, and follow- through."**

When my business was in its infancy in the early 2000s, I was facing "growing pains" and trying to overcome the challenges of growing a team and a start-up business. During that time, Wayne's words were pivotal in reminding me where and how to maintain focus.

Heck, even today, sixteen years later, this quote serves me well as I now lead a team of over 40 people and serve thousands of clients annually.

6. **You always do your best . . . and you never give up.**

Like all the aforementioned folks who failed miserably countless times over, you must be willing to put your successes and failures on the line.

Remember this, it is in the tough times that your BELIEFS will most be challenged. For me, it was during my toughest times that my FAITH and confidence were rattled—my dad's death. My back pain. Ken Sawyer's death.

The bottom line is that you dig deep, you keep fighting, you do your best, and you do NOT give up.

And so it is with you. Adhere to these six principles and watch your BELIEF and success soar like an eagle.

 ACTION STEP

Where can you risk greater in your life? What action steps can you take now to allow you to step outside of your comfort zone?

It is said that you must "Get comfortable being uncomfortable." Where can you demonstrate more risk, faith, and even failure in your life? After all, success is found in taking great steps forward—and that sometimes requires you even to **FAIL FORWARD**.

WOW NOTE: If you would like more information on Wayne Cotton's "7 Fs," I have supplied you with a special 2-page report from Wayne on exactly how you can live with more focus, faith, forward motion, and follow-through. Go to www.ToddDurkin.com/WOWBook-WayneCotton.

WOW 24
A DOG'S LIFE

My wife, Melanie, and I had our first "child" in 1998. Well, not really, but that's when Sid came into our lives.

He was just eight weeks old and was the cutest golden fluff of Golden Retriever you could ever imagine. Since we had no kids at the time, he really was like an only child.

We had so many great memories with him. Trips to the beach. Trips to the mountains and snow. Him hanging out at Fitness Quest 10 when we first opened in 2000. Sid meeting his three "younger" brothers and sister when they were born into the world—Luke, Brady, and McKenna.

Sid lived to be fifteen years old. And he helped create many fond memories and offered us a ton of love. I've often joked that he was the glue that kept our family together when we stressed from having kids, a growing business, and a busy lifestyle. While that's not completely true, Sid sure was special to us.

When he passed in 2013, someone sent us a sympathy card with a special quote about lessons we can learn from dogs that just made me smile.

And this is what it said:

DOGS

When loved ones come home, you always run to greet them.

You never pass up the opportunity to go for a joyride.

You allow the experience of fresh air and the wind in your face to be pure ecstasy.

You take naps.

You stretch before rising.

You run, romp, and play daily.

You thrive on attention and let people touch you.

You avoid biting when a simple growl will do.

On warm days, you stop to lie on your back on the grass.

On hot days, you drink lots of water and lie under a shady tree.

When you're happy, you dance around and wag your entire body.

You delight in the simple joy of a long walk.

You are loyal.

You never pretend to be something you're not.

If what you want lies buried, you dig until you find it.

When someone is having a bad day, you are silent, sit close by, and nuzzle them gently.

ACTION STEP

Choose at least one of these lessons that dogs teach us and write it down. And then apply it this week.

Thanks for all the lessons, Sid. You will forever be in our hearts!

WOW 25

BREATHE

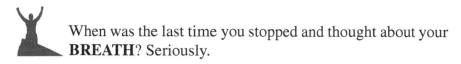 When was the last time you stopped and thought about your **BREATH**? Seriously.

And have you ever thought just how important **BREATH** is to performance? In sports? In work? In theater? In all aspects of life?

I was teaching a workshop to several hundred trainers one weekend, and afterwards an attendee asked a great question.

Since I had mentioned **BREATH** briefly in my talk, she asked, "How do you specifically address **BREATH** in a session? Or are there exercises you can do to help with this? And WHY should you do it?"

In my lecture, I talked about how the core of the human body worked in conjunction with the diaphragm. And how the diaphragm controls the breath. And I shared that the average person **BREATHES** 18,000 to 22,000 times per day.

And then I asked, "When was the last time you ever gave thanks for **BREATH**? When was the last time you even addressed your own **BREATH**?"

First off, breathwork is important for everyone. I shared that the average person **BREATHES** 18,000 to 22,000 times per day. And that same person often fails to EVER stop and think about **BREATH**, acknowledge **BREATH**, or work on **BREATH**.

As a matter of fact, the only time you often think about **BREATH** is when you're "out of **BREATH**."

Therefore, the first thing I encourage is AWARENESS. Just be aware of your breath. You can take a few minutes in the early morning to LISTEN to yourself **BREATHE**. Breath represents life. Give thanks. **BREATH**. MEDITATE. PRAY. Get quiet time. It's amazing what a few minutes of breathwork early in the morning will do for your entire day. Before your day actually gets going.

WHY?

From a performance perspective, **BREATH** is critical. If an athlete (at ANY level) gets tight, nervous, and anxious, and the breath becomes shallow, it does NOT matter how good a shape you're in. It doesn't matter how much you can squat. Or bench. Or how far you can push a heavy sled.

If the sympathetic nervous system is overloaded and the **BREATH** begins to become rapid and shallow (or you even hyper-ventilate), the body will become tight and constricted. Regardless of how good a shape you are in.

And you will NOT be able to perform at your optimum.

I often think back to my own competitive days as an athlete. In some of my biggest games, the first few were always ones where I sometimes felt like I was so out of shape. What was really happening was that I was so hyped and full of adrenaline that I would practically hyperventilate. That's not good.

Imagine that in front of 60,000 people as an NFL athlete. Or as a freshman in high school, starting for the varsity for the first time.

We need to learn how to control **BREATH.**

It's the same thing with the everyday desk jockey, executive, or person under stress. Breathwork is critical to relax the body and calm the mind.

So that's WHY breathwork is important.

"And HOW do you incorporate breathwork?" was the other part of the initial question I was asked.

First, you just learn how to be AWARE of **BREATH**. You do this by taking quiet time in the morning to LISTEN to your **BREATH**. Or after a workout.

And second, you take the time to actually do **BREATHING** exercises.

Some of us are under the gun with making big business decisions. **BREATHE**.

Some of us are facing challenges with life, family, and/or health. **BREATHE**.

Remember, **BREATH** represents LIFE. Take the time to be grateful for the many blessings we do have. It's easy when things are going smoothly. It's difficult when things are tough. But that's when it's actually imperative.

So today and this week, focus on **BREATHING**. Maybe it's early in the morning. Maybe it's taking a yoga class. Maybe it's investing five minutes after a hard workout that leaves you "**BREATHLESS**." Maybe it's listening to a meditation recording. Or journaling. The point is—**BREATHE**.

ACTION STEP

Sit comfortably or lie down for five minutes. And just be aware of your **BREATH**.

You are going to do a 4–5–6 BREATH. BREATHE in for a 4-count, hold your BREATH for a 5-count, and then exhale deeply for a 6-count. Do this for at least five minutes, and see how much more relaxed you feel.

The more you do this, the better.

Remember to LISTEN to your **BREATH** throughout the day, every day. It will tell you a lot.

And always be GRATEFUL for **BREATH**, as it represents LIFE. And for that we are extremely thankful.

PS: Go to www.ToddDurkin.com/WOWBook-1Better to get your free guided meditation to help you BREATHE!

WOW 26

212°

The year was 2009, and I had just started training Charles "Peanut" Tillman. Charles was a defensive back for the Chicago Bears at the time and was coming off his seventh year in the NFL. Unfortunately, he was coming off a tough year.

As a matter of fact, it was so bad that on ESPN one commentator ridiculed Charles, saying, "Oh, man. Peanut's getting roasted again." As if that were funny.

And then in the off-season, someone gifted Charles the book *212°: The Extra Degree* by Sam Parker.

The crux of the book is this:

At 211 degrees, water is hot, but nothing happens.

At **212 degrees**, water boils.

And with boiling water, comes steam.

And steam can power a locomotive.

It's all about that **ONE EXTRA** degree. In all you do.

For "Peanut," that one extra degree meant a lot of things—

Hiring a trainer (me), in addition to his team activities.

Improving his nutrition.

Improving his recovery and sleep habits.

Starting a foundation and giving back.

So how did all of this extra "heat" work out for Tillman? Did he bring the hot water to a roaring boil? Steam that locomotive? Absolutely. Peanut Tillman was a 15-year NFL veteran and was the 2013 Walter Payton NFL Man of the Year. I guess you can say he epitomizes "**212°**."

Sometimes life isn't going your way. Sometimes you need to go beyond, reach outside your comfort zone, and do things that scare you a bit.

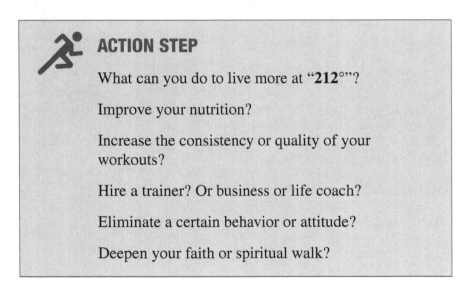

ACTION STEP

What can you do to live more at "**212°**"?

Improve your nutrition?

Increase the consistency or quality of your workouts?

Hire a trainer? Or business or life coach?

Eliminate a certain behavior or attitude?

Deepen your faith or spiritual walk?

Get it done TODAY and start to live at **212°**!

WOW 27

DO THE RIGHT THING!

Where your attention goes . . . Your energy flows.

Recently, I heard a particularly good story about a local athlete. He came to San Diego to play college football, but when he was 18, he worked for his hometown car dealership selling cars. One day, a family arrived on the used car lot looking for a van. The kids went nuts over a kitted out family van (TVs in the back, great stereo . . . you know what I mean), and the whole family was sold on it. When it came time to negotiate the final selling price, the father shooed everyone from the room and turned to our young athlete friend, man-to-man. He confided, "I need to buy a car today. I can buy this van for my family, but if I do, I'm going to be pinched so tight, I won't survive financially. If you bring the price down enough, I can swing it. Please help me if you can."

Now, this is where it started to get a little complicated. You see, this young man selling cars was pretty darned good at his job. He was so good that he was on the verge of winning a contest at the dealership that would earn him a $1,000 bonus. All he needed to win was to sell this one last car without allowing the price to dip much under sticker.

He immediately saw the dilemma. On the one hand, he could be a tough negotiator: sell high, win the contest, and bring home a great commission from the sale plus the contest prize money. This young man knew how to close a deal. He hadn't come this close to winning the contest without some significant selling ability. On the other hand, he was no stranger to financial hardship. He had grown up watching his own mom and dad worry about how they would pay the bills. He had some idea of the pressure this family was under. He could allow the negotiation to favor the family: give up most of his commission, lose the contest, lose the prize money, but know that he helped a family in need when they needed it most. What should he do?

What would you do?

Well, our young car salesman chose to place the needs of this family before his own. He remembered clearly how his parents had taught him to help others when he could—to recognize need and to respond. To give. To care. He dropped the price. He gave up his commission, lost the chance to win the contest, and watched a very happy family joyfully drive off the lot in their "new" van.

It's a good day's work, when payment comes from knowing you gave something of your own to help another. I loved this story. Eighteen years old is young. Not many 18 year olds would be so giving.

But there's more to the story. When the family drove away, the father said that he would send everyone he knew to this dealership and to this young salesman (do you think everyone who gets such a sweetheart deal likely says the same thing?). Later that same day, a man arrived at the dealership and insisted that the only person he could talk to was our young athlete friend. He introduced himself and said, "My brother-in-law bought a van from you this morning, and he told me how well you treated him. He told me I had to come in and ask for you." The man ended up purchasing a brand-new truck. And guess what folks—there was a different contest that our young salesman didn't know about. The purchase of this truck put him in first place and rewarded him with a $1,500 bonus plus his commission on the sale.

Call it karma. Call it what you want, but I believe that when we put positive energy out there, it flows back around to us. *Remember, where your attention goes, your energy flows.* When's the last time you gave something of yourself? When's the last time you walked away from a possible reward, so you could *help another . . . show a kindness . . . make a difference* for someone else?

ACTION STEP

This month, this week, TODAY, challenge yourself to do something meaningful for another person. Give of yourself: your time, your attention, your treasures, your wisdom. Surprise a loved one. Surprise a stranger. I'm betting it will be the highpoint of your day.

WOW 28

CRACKLINS, CRAWDADS & BOUDIN

It was 2014, and I was down in Lafayette, Louisiana, to speak to the American Heart Association and then do a half-day "IMPACT Leadership" program for a private company specializing in oil and gas industry transportation. And a funny thing happened once I landed at the airport.

I grabbed a taxi to shuttle to my hotel, and the driver asked with a deep Southern accent, "S-i-i-r-r-r . . . WHY are you here in Louisiana?"

I replied, "I'm here to speak at an American Heart Association function and for another group. I'm going to light a spark under their backsides and try to get the people down here healthier and more fit."

Looking at me through his rearview mirror, again he said with his long drawl, "Siirr . . . that should be real easy down here. You just have to tell everyone this . . .

"Tell them to stop eating boudin, cracklins, crawdads, gumbo soup, and turtle soup. That stuff's a delicacy down here and one of the reasons why many of us are overweight and not too healthy."

I stopped him and asked, "Ugh . . . sir, what is 'boo-dan' and cracklins?"

My driver, now with a big smile on his face, explained that boudin is like stuffed sausage filled with pork and heart meats. Cracklins are bits of fried pork skin.

My mouth just dropped, and I said, "Wow . . . they really eat that down here?"

He just smiled and about started salivating. And I just smiled and about got sick.

"This is EXACTLY what I'm going to tell the people to STOP eating!" I decided.

* * *

Sounds easy to do, right? Stop eating this . . . Stop eating that . . . Do this . . . Do that . . .

Right this minute, I could tell you 25 things you should stop eating. And 25 things you should start eating.

I could tell you 25 things to stop doing. And 25 things to start doing to get healthy.

But it probably wouldn't make a difference. Unless you want to make a change . . . like *really*, *really* want to **change**.

Every bit of knowledge you have and every bit of knowledge I have won't make a difference. We are NOT hurting for information.

But we are hurting for more discipline. For more accountability. For more willpower. These are the ingredients in the proven recipe to **CHANGE** unhealthy habits.

And this is what I want to talk with you about today—**CHANGE**—as it relates to life. Business. Exercise. Nutrition. Leadership. Relationships. Yourself.

You know what they say about **change**: **change** is inevitable. I often say, "Either you choose **change** . . . or **change** chooses you."

Sometimes **CHANGE** chooses you.

This could mean your unhealthy ways have caught up to you, and you now have heart disease. Or you have type 2 diabetes. Hypertension. Joint pain. Depression. Sadly, this list could go on and on.

Or, maybe it has nothing to do with your lifestyle, and you have just been diagnosed with cancer. Or you've had an accident or are facing a debilitating injury.

Or, maybe it's just life.

- Your spouse or significant other is offered an amazing job 3,000 miles away.

- Your landlord raises your rent beyond your ability to pay.

- Your biggest client no longer wants to do business with you.

- Your favorite trainer leaves the neighborhood gym you love.

- Your house has termites, and the bill is thousands of dollars.

- Your employer announces they are closing your office.

- Your last child is leaving the nest at the end of summer.

Change WILL happen. Again and again and again. We don't always like it. But we accept it because it's part of life. Like the ocean tides coming in and going out.

I believe there are energy shifts at different times in a person's life. And the most important thing each of us can do is to honor that energy by **preparing for change**. Nurture your best practices and disciplines to grow personally and professionally. Be READY.

So, my friend, where do you stand today on **CHANGE** in your life? Are you prepared for the next high tide?

Choose **CHANGE** today!

Are you, right now, living the healthiest you? Check in on the following:

- Your overall fitness levels and conditioning

- Your flexibility and how good your body FEELS

- Your body composition or how your body LOOKS

- Your biometrics (blood pressure, cholesterol, waist/hip ratio, blood panel, etc.)

- Your living environment

- Your work environment

- Who you surround yourself with

- A specific relationship you are in

Added together, these make up the healthiest you. So remember, you are in the driver's seat. You can choose **change** before it chooses you. You can choose to be ready. To live your healthiest life.

This kind of **change** doesn't need to be massive to make a big difference. Sometimes it's just a matter of getting your mind right and choosing a different perspective.

For some, **change** might need to be BIG, but the first step never is. Begin where you can. **Change** of all sizes requires courage. Have the courage to **CHANGE** what needs to change in your life.

And whether your greatest needs are physical, mental, emotional, spiritual, environmental, professional, or personal—**choose change for a healthier you**.

ACTION STEP

Choose what you want to **change** in your life. Write it down, share it with someone close to you, and then make it happen. No more excuses. Get it done!

WOW 29

MOM

There's a story behind everyone . . . and behind your story is always your mother's story . . . because hers is where yours begins.
—Mitch Albom, Writer

Mom. What a sweet word. It conjures up such sweet thoughts, feelings, and emotions.

Being the youngest of eight kids, I have eight words/thoughts that come to mind when I think of my mom.

1. **Grateful**

   I'm grateful that my mom is still living. She's 82 years old and lives in Orlando, Florida. There isn't a day that goes by that I'm not thankful that I can still call her or hug/hold her when I see her. She's in relatively good health, and she still travels around quite a bit to see all her "kids" and grandkids.

2. **Persistence**

   We never had it easy growing up. My mom had eight kids. I'm the youngest of my five sisters and two brothers. She and my dad divorced when I was just five. We didn't have much money. I was a "lunch ticket" kid (you may only know what that is and how embarrassing it is if you had to buy your school lunches with subsidized funds). She had to sell our house where all eight kids grew up when I was in the eighth grade. She needed to get money to pay the bills, so

125

she moved us into a "rental home" down the street. With all of this, Mom was extremely resilient and persistent. And she was one tough cookie. Always.

3. Radiant

Despite our adversity, Mom never complained. As a matter of fact, it was quite the opposite. You see, I didn't know any different when I was young that we didn't have a lot of money or that *this* wasn't normal. And that's because Mom was always smiling with radiant energy. She made me feel special. She made me feel loved and cared for. She was a beautiful woman. And still is!

4. Positive

She didn't complain. She didn't gossip. She always only said nice things about people. She has always been one of the most positive people I know.

She always said, "If you don't have something nice to say about someone, then don't say it."

5. Loving

I guess moms are "supposed" to be loving, right? I guess so. But it's not always easy, and it's the little things that she did for me when I was young that I most appreciate.

- The laundry *every* night after Pop Warner and high school football, basketball, and baseball practices. *Every* night. For many, many years.

- Having the large box of Honey Nut Cheerios in the cupboard that I ate every morning. *Every* morning.

- Her staying within the Brick High School zone when we had to move so that I could play football for Coach Wolf.

• And the list goes on an on.

Little things. But BIG things when you're a kid. And I appreciate it as much today as I did back then.

There was a little saying that hung on the wall in the house I grew up in on 13 Edgewood Drive: "A man works from sun to sun . . . but a woman's work is never done."

Thank you, Mom, for all you did.

6. Selfless

In 1994, my mom had been left a little bit of "angel" money from a woman that she had been a caretaker of for many years. My mom could have lived off that money for many years. Instead, she decided to take our entire family (twenty-seven people, including nephews/nieces) on an all-expense-paid cruise to Bermuda. Her thought, "I want my entire family all together locked on a ship for one week before I die." And that's WHY she did it!

7. Adventurous

Mom, especially in the last twenty years of her life, has been quite the traveler. She's been on numerous vacations, trips, and cruises since that Bermuda trip, including trips to France and Greece. I think it was that Bermuda trip that catapulted her adventurous spirit, and she's been having fun ever since.

And the fact that the "kids" are all grown now, we have been able to "repay" her for the many sacrifices she made for so many years.

Mom now loves bopping around the country to see all her children in New Jersey, Texas, Florida, and California—and she's always up for a cruise if someone's going!

8. Grateful

Did I already say that? Oh yeah, I started with that one. And I choose to end with it again. Because seriously, I'm so grateful for my mom. For the sacrifices she made, for what she did, and who she is today.

I started with Mitch Albom's words:

There's a story behind everyone . . . and behind your story is always your mother's story . . . because hers is where yours begins.

I know everyone has their own unique stories of their mom. And I would love to hear them.

Where does your story begin? WHO is your mom?

And if there is one word (or eight!) or character trait that most defines your mom or that you most LOVE about your mom, please share it on the WOW Book Facebook page. I want to read WHO the person behind your story is.

ACTION STEP

The WOW is the one word that best describes your Mom, whether she's living or has passed.

And whatever that one word to BEST describe your Mom is, that is your WOW. Maybe it's persistence. Or radiance. Or patience. Or happy. Or positive. Or any word that comes to mind.

For me, that one word I will most live by this week that epitomizes my mom is LOVE!

Thanks, Mom. I love you.

PS: Please share that ONE word that most defines your mom over on the WOW Book Facebook page. Just be sure to put #WowMom after it!

Thanks for sharing.

WOW 30
DEWEY BOZELLA

His name is Dewey Bozella, and he fought his very first professional boxing match on October 15, 2011. He won. Dewey Bozella was 52 years old in his debut.

Yes, my friend, that's correct. At 52 years of age, Dewey Bozella finally had the chance to live his dream—the dream to be a professional boxer—the dream that kept him going for most of his life. You see, for 26 years, Dewey lived behind bars for a murder he didn't commit. Several times he was offered a plea bargain. Freedom—if only he would say he was guilty.

According to Dewey, he would rather "rot in jail" than say he did it. More than once he made the painful decision to refuse the plea. An innocent man in prison for 26 years. No stranger to pain. His father beat his pregnant mother to death when he was only nine years old, and two of his brothers were murdered on the streets of Brooklyn while he was just a teen. This man's entire life was filled with pain.

Twenty-six years is nearly 10,000 days. All that time Dewey dreamt and worked for one thing: the day he would walk away from prison a free man and have the chance to fight as a professional boxer. In 2009, justice was served, and he did walk away free. He was exonerated of the crime after a quarter of a century spent trying to prove his innocence.

What a path to travel to **achieve your dream!**

Dewey Bozella fought Larry Hopkins on the undercard of a Bernard

Hopkins (no relation to Larry Hopkins) fight. Dewey won by a unanimous decision and immediately afterward shared, "I used to lie in my cell and dream about this day happening. It was all worth it. It is my dream come true. This is my first and last fight . . . I did what I wanted to do, and I'm happy." He fought. He won. And then he retired when **his dream was realized**.

My friend, what about **you and your dreams**? Likely, you aren't in prison. Likely, you haven't faced the battles Dewey faced. But each of us has walked a unique path to arrive where we are today. We've faced challenges and struggled through adversity. And now, more than ever, our dreams are so important because **dreams do keep us alive**. They **empower** and **motivate** us. They give us **purpose** and put **meaning** into every day and every action. Dewey Bozella got up each day for 26 years and **lived with purpose**. He never gave up—and neither should you.

Let your dreams do their magic. Allow them to fuel your day, give you energy, and keep you focused. They'll do all this and more. It doesn't matter if it takes 6 months, 6 years, or 26 years to achieve, never give up. You've got to **make your dreams come true.**

Dewey Bozella is an amazing example of someone who very easily could have given up many times. Can you imagine nearly 10,000 days of wrongful imprisonment? He could have lived with rage. He could have lived with anger. He could have lived with hatred. He could have given up on any one of those 10,000 days. But that's the thing that makes Dewey Bozella so special. He didn't. Instead, he **CHOSE** to live with **PURPOSE**. He chose to **DREAM**.

What a great lesson this man is for all of us. Regardless of circumstance, hardships, turmoil, adversity, or situation, choose to keep fighting. Choose to keep **persisting**. Choose to keep **believing**. And always choose to keep **DREAMING**.

After all, **dreams can come true**!

Thanks, Dewey Bozella, for never conceding, always believing—and ultimately living out your dreams!

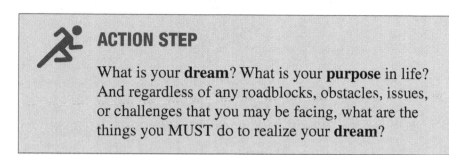

ACTION STEP

What is your **dream**? What is your **purpose** in life? And regardless of any roadblocks, obstacles, issues, or challenges that you may be facing, what are the things you MUST do to realize your **dream**?

Never give up faith, keep dreaming, and always believe in YOU!

WOW 31
1% BETTER

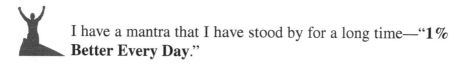 I have a mantra that I have stood by for a long time—"**1% Better Every Day**."

I live by this mindset. I love it. It drives me to be better. Every. Single. Day.

This mantra simply is a reminder to me that we should strive for progress every day and seek continual improvement. And it helps me focus on just "winning the day."

This mindset is also part of what's called the "Growth Mindset." Always looking to get better and improve our lives. If you are reading this, you probably understand exactly what I'm talking about. Progress is the name of the game.

And we can seek **PROGRESS** in many different areas of our lives:

- **Progress** with our personal health, fitness, nutrition, or conditioning.

- **Progress** in business.

- **Progress** in a career.

- **Progress** in relationships.

- **Progress** with a big project you are working on.

- **Progress** with a book you are writing. Or a blog, website, social media presence. On a presentation that you need to create. On a proposal you are working on.

- **Progress** with a certain skill you are trying to develop or master.

- **Progress** with your spiritual walk.

- **Progress** with . . . (you fill in the blank).

Life is about **progress**. Little steps every single day that will ultimately help get you to where you want to go.

Does that mean you are NOT going to have adversity, trials, tribulations, obstacles, and issues that pop up in your life? Absolutely not. Quite the contrary.

YOU WILL face all of these. As a matter of fact, I can say you will face all of these . . . and then some. But it is from these adversities and obstacles, when you navigate through them, that you make massive amounts of **PROGRESS**.

For example, one of my personal goals is to take at least 10 minutes of "quiet time" first thing every morning to nourish and feed my soul. This could come in the form of praying, journaling, or reading the Bible BEFORE I work out.

I am NOT always great at consistently taking those 10 minutes. But I always get in my workout time.

However, since my goal is to dive in even deeper spiritually, I recently committed to getting in that "10-minute power hour" first thing in the morning AND then listening to a spirit-enriching, soul-empowering podcast for at least 30 minutes during my workout to feed my mind, body, and spirit.

This is an example of **1% Better Every Day**.

If I get in my 10 minutes of quiet time AND listen to my podcast while working out—watch out world, here I come. If I don't . . . just watch out!

How about you? Where can you improve in your life? Or in your business? How can you make the most important changes that you want and need in your life to bring you the most fulfillment and happiness?

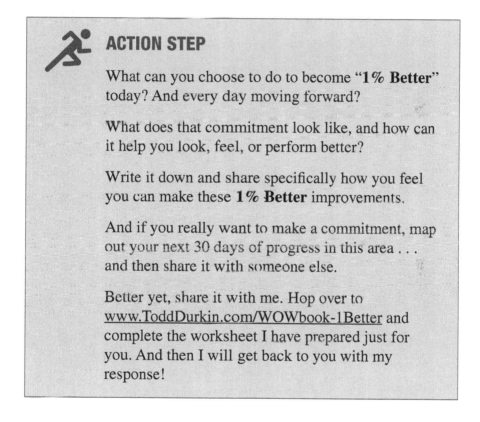

ACTION STEP

What can you choose to do to become **"1% Better"** today? And every day moving forward?

What does that commitment look like, and how can it help you look, feel, or perform better?

Write it down and share specifically how you feel you can make these **1% Better** improvements.

And if you really want to make a commitment, map out your next 30 days of progress in this area . . . and then share it with someone else.

Better yet, share it with me. Hop over to www.ToddDurkin.com/WOWbook-1Better and complete the worksheet I have prepared just for you. And then I will get back to you with my response!

Dig your teeth into where you need to focus your attention today and then get it done. After all, **1% Better** is a mindset to help you succeed and be your best. And I'm here to help you do that. Let's GO!

1% Better

And keep that mantra going in your mind . . .

1% Better

1% Better

1% Better

And watch what happens in as little as 30-days: BOOM. **IMPACT!**

WOW 32

GOOD NEWS TRAIN

Enough already! I'm tired of people telling me how bad things are out there. All you read and hear about is how the world is in financial ruin, people are losing their jobs and their homes, and everyone's stress levels and body weights are higher than ever.

I hear FEAR in people's voices. I'm surrounded by negative attitudes, and it's time to stop.

Listen, I get it. I'm not in denial. But it's time to turn this around, stop worrying about what you can't control, and start taking action on what YOU CAN.

If Franklin Delano Roosevelt was right and "the only thing we have to fear is fear itself," then let's start dealing with the problem. Don't let fear take over. Lift yourself up. Fight back. Begin by creating a filter for all this bad news. Keep a check on how much you take in, and remember that the best antidote to bad news is **good news**—so start to surround yourself with it.

Take control of your life and begin to capture some of the **"goodness"** around you. In my professional world of fitness, health, and performance, I know and respect the power of mental attitude. If it's a struggle for you to say no to all this fear, then "fake it till you make it." Look for the positive, create **good news**, and do whatever it takes to hang onto hope.

Here are several ways you can positively affect your body, mind, and attitude to protect yourself against the negative forces that exist today.

- **Make a commitment to your physical conditioning**. Set goals, hire a trainer, go outdoors and enjoy nature, try new classes, like Pilates or yoga, and improve your nutrition. There is nothing like the feeling of a euphoric workout when endorphins are released. Commit to your physical conditioning and watch how it positively affects your mindset, attitude, and overall health. Do something every day for YOU! It's the best investment you can ever make.

- **Get a massage**. Just like a great workout, a therapeutic massage can melt away stress and anxiety. A great massage from a qualified therapist can correct muscle imbalances, improve flexibility, assist with recovery, reduce pain, and help you feel better physically and mentally. While a massage a week is ideal, even receiving one per month can help improve your physical and mental health and well-being.

- **Invest in your spiritual life**. I was talking to a client recently who gets up at 4:30 am everyday to spend 45 minutes with his daily devotion, journaling, and prayer time before hitting the gym at 5:30 am. He does this at least five days a week. I thought to myself, "Talk about fortifying your armor for the day—this is the best way to start." When the mind, body, and spirit are all nourished, balance and harmony are in place, and you are ready to take on each day, regardless of how big the challenge.

- **Solve a problem**. Free yourself from a nagging problem. At Fitness Quest 10, we are in the business of helping clients to solve problems. We may not be mortgage brokers or bankers, career counselors or investment advisors, but we are in the business of helping others to achieve goals. Regularly, I hear from clients who have been suffering from an old injury or weakness and when combined with the rising stresses of daily life, the pain and discomfort are more than they can manage. If this describes you, are you finally willing to get some help? Some problems can be solved with bodywork, some with chiropractic or physical therapy, and some require a more serious medical consult. Make a commitment and get to the bottom of the issue—starting today.

- **Simplify your life**. Eliminate extraneous stressors. One person's *extra* might be another's *essential*, but take a careful look at where your time and money go. Cut out some of the fat to reduce the drain on your wallet and your energy. Focus on greater personal and professional gain. Start to enjoy more quality time spent with friends and loved ones. I recently heard of one family who sacrificed their weekly date night and substituted it with a nightly trip to the hot tub after the kids were in bed. The savings were as much as $400 a month, and they were enjoying the benefit of quiet talk time every week.

- **"Protect this house."** At Under Armour, this tagline is used to talk about protecting the brand. I am using this line to talk about protecting your "house"—your mindset! You can filter what you listen to, what you read, whom you talk to, and how you spend your time. "Protect your house" by reading great books, listening to great programs, avoiding negative people, and being very selective in how you spend your time and with whom you spend it.

- **Don't live in FEAR!** Listen, we all have fears. High performers don't let fears guide their decisions or affect their actions. The hardest part of achieving any goal or desire is often getting started. As Franklin Roosevelt advised, "The best way to tackle fear is to tackle the things you fear the most." If you are living paralyzed by all the "what ifs" in your life, address them head-on. Educate yourself, seek professional counsel, and make a plan. "Stop the bleed" and begin to channel that anxious energy toward your future. Take action to begin building momentum on the things you are passionate and enthusiastic about in life. Now might be the time to be confident in your instincts. This might be your opportunity to build or to invest in something you believe in. This is the time when leaders take initiative.

- **Find the good in everyone and everything.** It's easy to find bad stuff out there, but even if it takes a little more effort, seek out the good. Especially now, beware of media hype—look for news sources that are committed to balance. Listen for reports of industries and businesses that do well in recession—not all the stories are about how business is booming for yacht repossession specialists in Boca Raton! My challenge to you is to find the good in everyone and everything.

There's a great saying among the twelve-step community, "Treat your mind like a dangerous neighborhood—never go there alone!" Try not to dwell on the bad news of today. When we let fear in, it can paralyze us. Remember, we are in this together, so let's make the best of it by catching the **"good news" train** and exercising the control we have.

I encourage you to stay focused on living in the moment and protecting your mindset from the toxic side effects of bad news. Invest in yourself, your physical health, your mental well-being, and your spiritual life. The payoff is big. You CAN control your environment, how you spend your time, and with whom you spend it. Guard yourself and continue to protect the most valuable assets you have—your physical, mental/emotional, and spiritual well-being. INVEST IN YOURSELF.

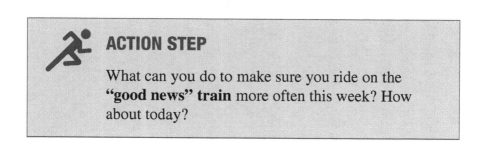

ACTION STEP

What can you do to make sure you ride on the **"good news" train** more often this week? How about today?

Make great choices today and go create and deliver **some great news!**

WOW 33

STONECUTTER

Sometimes life's challenges get in the way of what we really want to accomplish.

Sometimes we dream big, get momentum going, and then face a major roadblock.

This short Indian fable has always stayed near and dear to my heart.

THE STONECUTTER

A stonecutter starts out with a big hammer and whacks a large rock as hard as he can, trying to split it. The first time he hits it, there's not even a scratch, not as much as a chip—absolutely nothing. He pulls back the hammer and unleashes another blow to the mighty stone again and again—100, 200, 500 times—and still nothing.

After all this effort, the boulder does not show even the slightest crack, but he keeps on hitting it anyway. People sometimes pass by and laugh at him for persisting when obviously his actions are having NO effect. But the stonecutter is very wise. He doesn't concern himself with what other people think.

He knows that just because you don't see immediate results from your current actions, it doesn't mean that you're not making any progress. He keeps hitting at different points in the stone, over and over again, relentless in his pursuit. At some point, possibly on the 800th or 900th hit, or quite possibly the 2,000th strike—the massive stone doesn't just chip, it literally SPLITS IN TWO.

Was it this one single hit that broke the stone in half? Of course not. It was the constant focus and consistent effort the stonecutter applied to the challenge at hand that created the ultimate result. The rock was conquered.

Here is the moral of the story: The consistent application and discipline of constant effort and never-ending improvement is the key to success. And the consistent swinging of the hammer, despite others' rebukes, proves that any boulder blocking the path to your progress can be broken in half.

So, where are you at in the pursuit of your dreams and goals?

Sometimes you can see the light at the end of the tunnel. And sometimes you can't.

Sometimes people will judge you and discourage you as you pursue your dreams and goals.

Regardless, you have to keep swinging your hammer!

Be a **STONECUTTER** today. Keep chopping!

ACTION STEP

What big project are you working on that you must continue chipping away at?

Spend at least thirty minutes a day chipping away at whatever it is you so desire.

Remember, success is many small efforts done well, over and over again. Be like the **STONECUTTER** and keep chipping away at it. And don't pay any attention to the naysayers. You are closer than you think to getting to where you want to go.

WOW 34

MASTERMIND

Your network is your net worth.
—Professor Howard Smith,
The College of William & Mary, circa 1993

I read Napoleon Hill's *Think and Grow Rich* book in 2005, and it changed my entire thought process on success.

Hill spoke about the power of collaboration and the power of a collective unit of successful mindsets that are geared to the same cause.

Essentially, he shared that your thought processes, idea streams, and heightened states of consciousness come from when you put yourself around other motivated, success-driven individuals. And it was the first time I had heard of the "**MASTERMIND**" concept.

So in 2005 I joined a **MASTERMIND** group of other fitness pros, led by a leading fitness entrepreneur named Phil Kaplan.

And then in 2006, I joined a **MASTERMIND** led by female entrepreneur-extraordinaire, Ali Brown. Ali was a gal who helped transform my on-line business, and I love her entrepreneurial spirit.

And then in 2007, I joined a **MASTERMIND** led by leadership expert, Robin Sharma. His coaching group was primarily on leadership and personal mastery. And I loved it and benefitted from it immensely.

And on October 15, 2007, I started the Todd Durkin **MASTERMIND**. Initially, this was a group of 12 fitness professionals who were yearning to get to the next level in their training businesses. We had monthly calls, webinars, and live meetings. I emailed group members regularly, and I did teleconference group coaching sessions. I LOVED IT!

Nine years later, my **MASTERMIND** has now grown to three different levels (Institute, Platinum, and Power of 10), and we have fitness professionals of all levels. And the focus is on business development, marketing, leadership, "in the trenches" acumen, and personal development.

And my **MASTERMIND** members truly INSPIRE me! They are some of the best of the best human beings on the planet. Seriously.

They are dedicated and inspired to make the world a better place. It's an honor to serve them. And they inspire ME more than they will ever know.

As Professor Howard Smith shared with me in my Kinesiology 408 class back many moons ago, "Your network is your net worth."

Think about the 5 closest people to you in your life. Who are they?

You are probably of the same socio-economic status and belief system as those 5 people. Do you like who you are hanging out with and spending time with?

If you want to be a great athlete—train with other great athletes.

If you want to be a great coach—learn from great coaches.

If you want to be a millionaire—hang out with millionaires.

If you want to be spiritually strong—hang out with spiritually strong people.

Bottom line is this . . . YOU are who you hang out with! So why not spend time with people who inspire you and bring out your best?

 ACTION STEP

Write down in your WOW journal the 5 closest people to you in your life.

Write down 3 people in your life that you would like to spend more time with (perhaps for business mentorship, personal development, social reasons, spiritual reasons, etc.).

How can you do a better job investing time with those closest to you in your life on a regular basis?

 WOW NOTE 1: New WOW Mastermind Group of NON-fitness pros soon forming!

Visit www.ToddDurkin.com/WOWBook-Mastermind on how you can get involved with our new "WOW Mastermind" for people from all walks of life. This is not just for fitness pros. This WOW Mastermind will be on training, nutrition, leadership, and personal mastery.

WOW NOTE 2: My Todd Durkin Mastermind for Fit-Pros has done some truly incredible things across the globe. To see just some of the group members' accomplishments, check out http://ToddDurkinMastermind.com.

WOW 35

HABITS

I love training athletes. Especially NFL athletes in June and July right before training camp. It's the four-week window when all the NFL athletes are making their final preparations for the upcoming season. It's the culmination of an off-season filled with training and OTAs (organized team activities) when dreams of a championship really start to brew.

For me, it's GO TIME. A "sprint" to get my guys ready physically and mentally for one of the more punishing sports on the planet.

And for every Drew Brees, Darren Sproles, Charles Tillman, Carson Palmer, Gerald McCoy, Zach Ertz, or Chase Daniel who comes through the doors to prepare to win a championship, there are many athletes who are fighting to put food on the table. To earn a spot on a team. And to have a career in the NFL.

Out of the hundreds of guys I have prepped each off-season for the past 15 years or so, there are 10 **habits** that are important to share with you if you are looking to maximize your performance. Take a look.

1. **Hard work and disciplined habits are crucial to success**.
   The guys train five days a week during this time. Some days are double sessions. We have weight room work, plus field work where we do movement training and all football-related work. We integrate Pilates into their routines and add massage and bodywork to help with recovery one or two times a week.

2. **Nutrition is critical!** Some guys are trying to gain weight. Some guys are trying to lose weight. Every one of them must focus on eating clean, high-quality foods. Each has specific needs and unique tastes. We always finish our sessions with a recovery shake that is 2:1 carbs to proteins, and each athlete has a specific supplement protocol they follow (some of the basic foundational ones I recommend are fish oils, multivitamin, BCAAs, and glutamine). I advocate nutrient timing and encourage them to eat every three hours to take in highly nutritious whole foods full of fiber, vitamins, and nutrients.

3. **Imbalances or weaknesses are corrected NOW**. Heck, even these athletes can have weaknesses. That's why we emphasize soft tissue work before a session. That's why we do a lot of flexibility work post-session. And it's why we incorporate Pilates, yoga, and bodywork into their programs. We do a ton of unilateral work in the weight room and emphasize the "back-side" of the body (the non-mirrored muscles!). But the message is the same for everyone who trains at FQ10: fight imbalances to help stave off injury and improve performance.

4. **Environment counts**. The energy at Fitness Quest 10 is always electric. And while we pride ourselves on high energy all the time, it turns up a few decibels in July. Think about it. Don't environment and energy play a critical role in the quality of your sessions and training? The music, the people you train with or around, the pulse, the vibe, the clanking of iron . . . Ah-h-h, it's summer time! From 7 year olds to 87 year olds to everyone in between, summer ratchets up the energy a few more notches for the Joes and the pros. I LOVE IT!

5. **Make the right CHOICES**. Closely related to "environment," the CHOICES made by each of my guys

outside the gym go a long way toward determining the outcome of their hard work. Yes, where you train, who you train with, what you eat, when you eat, and how you recover are key, but there's more. Who you spend time with, who you socialize with, what you watch on TV, what you read—ALL of this counts, and they know it.

6. **GET YOUR MIND RIGHT**. Some guys are stars in the league. Some guys are backups. Some guys are "bubble" guys. And some are still trying to hold onto the dream. Each MUST HAVE A STEADFAST BELIEF in himself and in his dream.

7. **Attention to DETAILS**. If you ever saw Darren Sproles practice on the field, you would see him run 40 yards down the field after EVERY catch he makes. And this is in PRACTICE. Yes, I said P-R-A-C-T-I-C-E! He's getting used to YAC (yards after the catch). And if you ever saw Drew Brees practicing his field work in July, you would see him work his mental checklist on a continuous loop. Over and over . . . his checks, his reads, and different scenarios he will face. The best of the best athletes are meticulous with attention to details. They practice the details in every training session because the details pay dividends come game day.

8. **FOCUS**. The NFL athletes are zeroed in right now. Focused like thoroughbreds ready to run the Kentucky Derby (or opening day at Del Mar!). When you know what you NEED to do and WANT to do and you are intensely FOCUSED on achieving that dream, anything is possible.

9. **Be humble. Be Hungry.** The athletes who come to Fitness Quest 10 are humble. They set great examples, they are great role models for our kids, and they fit right into the positive culture in the Fitness Quest 10 DNA. These guys are also incredibly hungry and work their tails off to be the best they

can be. It shows up in how they train, in how they practice, and how they play on Sundays. This is a combination that is unbeatable.

10. **1% Better Every Day.** My late-friend Ken Sawyer lived by a mantra called "DO BETTER" (see Wow 3 and Wow 31). With the mindset and attitude for continual improvement, our athletes pursue excellence every day.

It all comes down to **HABITS** and **BEST PRACTICES**. I wanted to share some of the best practices I see from behind the scenes, working with some of the best athletes in the world. But this list is not only for athletes. If YOU train and live with the same discipline, the same work ethic, and the same mindset, you WILL see great results. Not only in your physical conditioning, but in your entire LIFE as well.

ACTION STEP

Take a couple of these key points from above and implement them yourself into your routine. They ALL count, and they pay great dividends.

And remember, when you are picking your fantasy teams this season, you can never go wrong picking a Fitness Quest 10 athlete!

WOW 36
PRECIOUS MOMENTS

 I love the quote, "Life is defined not by the number of breaths you take, but by the moments that take your breath away."

When my daughter McKenna was in kindergarten, I had one of those magical moments that lasts a lifetime.

It was the father-daughter dance, and we were both so looking forward to going to it.

McKenna primped all afternoon with my wife, Melanie. They got flowers for her hair. McKenna picked out her favorite "fancy dress" and looked adorable when she was ready to go.

I got my suit pressed, my dozen roses and corsage ordered, and wrote a little note to McKenna letting her know how much I was looking forward to our time together.

As we drove over to the venue, we listened to our favorite song, Jersey Boys' "My Eyes Adored You."

She shared that she was a little nervous going to her first dance. But her butterflies soon subsided as we walked in, and she saw a bunch of her friends.

And while there were many great parts to the night, here was perhaps the most **PRECIOUS** one.

The dance ran from 6 to 8 pm. We were dancing away on the floor after dinner when McKenna just looked at me and said, "Daddy, I'm really tired, can we go home now?"

I looked at my watch, and it was just 7 pm.

I looked at her little, round, sleepy eyes, and you could tell that her bedtime had hit. She looked so tired. My little, precious princess was exhausted, and she wanted to get going home.

I just smiled and said, "Of course, McKenna. Let's get going." She was in bed before 8 pm, and I tucked her in and just smiled.

Life is defined by the precious moments that take your breath away. And this was one of them.

We were only at the dance about an hour. We had a great time, but my five-year-old couldn't fight being tired any longer.

For those of you with older kids, I am constantly reminded of how quickly the time passes by. I get it. I see it. I understand it.

And it was just so awesome to be present in this moment with my little girl and know how quickly this time would pass.

On the drive home, I could see her tired eyes getting heavier and heavier. And I thought about our upcoming dances. I thought about how someday, God willing, I will see her get married. And I realized how quickly that day would be here.

Truly a **PRECIOUS** moment.

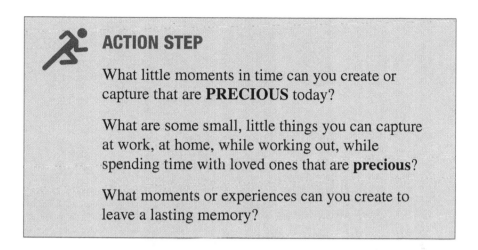

ACTION STEP

What little moments in time can you create or capture that are **PRECIOUS** today?

What are some small, little things you can capture at work, at home, while working out, while spending time with loved ones that are **precious**?

What moments or experiences can you create to leave a lasting memory?

They don't all have to be "big" things. They don't have to be dances. Or weddings. Or big vacation getaways.

Serve others, slow down enough to be present in all conversations, put a smile on someone else's face, teach or coach someone something new, or create experiences that will make a difference in other people's lives.

Now that would be **PRECIOUS**!

Thank you, McKenna, for reminding me that great things come in small, **precious** packages. You just got to keep your eyes open to capture the moments—even when they can't.

WOW 37
RECHARGE

 It's amazing what even twenty-four hours away will do for the soul. My wife, Melanie, and I got away for a night to a day spa called Two Bunch Palms to **RECHARGE**.

On the drive out to the desert, Melanie and I got so immersed in conversation that I literally went twenty-five miles past the exit I was supposed to turn off on. And instead of a two-hour drive, it turned into a three-hour journey.

We both laughed, saying, "We must have really needed to talk!"

Heck, it shows you how much even just a good drive can do for communication with the spouse. We talked kids, relationship, work, dreams . . . and the next thing I knew I was seeing signs for Phoenix, Arizona. Uh-oh.

Man, having that driving time with Melanie was one of my highlights.

Lounging in the "grotto" pool, hot tub, "cold" pool, eating together, yoga, getting body treatments, and time away were all fantastic also.

I turned off my phone on Saturday afternoon and didn't turn it on until Sunday afternoon.

Try doing that—twenty-four hours of DISCONNECTING. No phone. No texting. No emailing. No tweeting. No Facebooking. No Instagramming. **100% RECHARGE** time.

Dang, it actually felt great. I could have used another week of it, but hey, I will take a day. Try it sometime and see how great you feel!

Let me just offer this.

We all need more "mellow-yellow" time. And it must be built into the calendar. I learned this from one of my mentors Wayne Cotton many years ago. I can't emphasize enough how important it is to schedule this **RECHARGE** time on your calendar. Now.

Maybe it's a one-day trip.

Maybe it's a long weekend.

Maybe it's a weeklong trip.

Or maybe you start to plan your "dream" trip for your future.

But get that "carrot" on the calendar NOW.

When we left the spa grounds, we felt great. My skin felt rejuvenated from the fresh mineral water in the pools, the massage, and all the relaxation. My head was clear, my face was relaxed, and my energy was vibrant. **RECHARGED**.

In today's hustle-and-bustle, busy world, we all need a good **RECHARGE** of the body, mind, and spirit. A drive in the car, getting into nature, getting some bodywork, disconnecting from technology, and tapping into your inner self—even for a night or two or three or more at a resort—can do wonders.

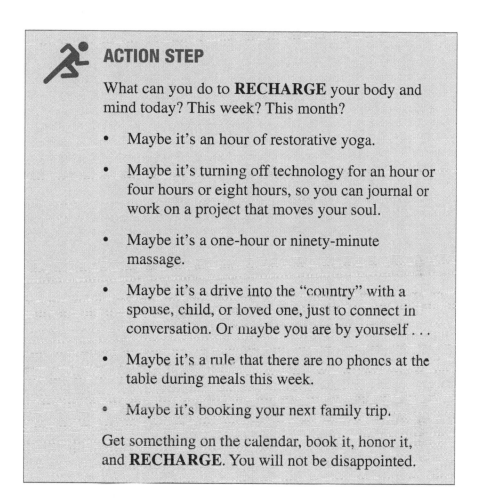

ACTION STEP

What can you do to **RECHARGE** your body and mind today? This week? This month?

- Maybe it's an hour of restorative yoga.

- Maybe it's turning off technology for an hour or four hours or eight hours, so you can journal or work on a project that moves your soul.

- Maybe it's a one-hour or ninety-minute massage.

- Maybe it's a drive into the "country" with a spouse, child, or loved one, just to connect in conversation. Or maybe you are by yourself . . .

- Maybe it's a rule that there are no phones at the table during meals this week.

- Maybe it's booking your next family trip.

Get something on the calendar, book it, honor it, and **RECHARGE**. You will not be disappointed.

Energy is everything. And in order to create and maintain positive energy, we all need to **RECHARGE** our batteries more often. Honor your energy and spirit each day. It is amazing what a **RECHARGE** does for your body, mind, and soul.

WOW 38
APPROACHABLE

I was walking through McCarran Airport in Las Vegas one evening, getting ready to depart on a flight after having taught at a fitness conference. As I was approaching my gate, a young gal (about twenty-five years old) stopped me literally in the middle of the walkway at the airport.

And she said, "You're Todd Durkin, right? I have read your *IMPACT Body Plan* book, I want to become a trainer, I follow your plan, I live by *IMPACT*, I follow your social media, and I'm a big fan. I'm in another field now but want to become a trainer."

I was like WOW. That's really cool. And in Vegas, of all places. I was very glad she stopped me and spoke to me. I felt like a rock star.

Truth is, many people within the fitness or sports-training industry may recognize me. But not a ton of folks outside of that.

So, man, it made me feel special to be recognized.

Later on the plane, I thought some more—

APPROACHABLE.

I wondered if clients felt like they could APPROACH me or my teammates when they had a question. Or if they had a problem.

I wondered if my team felt like they could APPROACH me if they had a question. Or wanted feedback. Or if they had a problem.

I wondered if my kids felt comfortable APPROACHING me to talk about ANYTHING.

Leaders are **APPROACHABLE**. This means warm, caring, genuine, truly interested, non-intimidating, and great listeners.

I hope that I'm always **APPROACHABLE**.

How about you? Are you **APPROACHABLE**?

ACTION STEP

What can you do to be more **APPROACHABLE** this week?

Who can you APPROACH this week and acknowledge, praise, or encourage?

And if you ever see me out and about, please APPROACH me. Let's get a picture together and spread some WOW across the universe.

WOW 39
CANDY & WILLPOWER

Could you give up candy for a year?

Or how about coffee? Or nicotine? Or wine? Or chocolate? Or TV? Or social media?

My son Luke gave up candy at the age of eleven for an entire year.

One entire year. 365 days. NO CANDY. NO SODA. Seriously.

As a kid, that is tough. Heck, as an adult, that would be tough.

And Luke did it. From April 1, 2014 to April 1, 2015 (no joke!).

That included Halloween. Birthday parties. A trip to Europe (man, the chocolate in Austria was delicious!). And any other day that his friends, brother, or sister ate candy in front of him.

And it was all of his own volition. His choice. His WILLPOWER.

You see, on April 1, 2014, my wife, Melanie, and he were in a discussion about a friend of his who had resolved to give up soda for a year. And that young man completed it.

So Luke said to his mom, "Mom, what will you give me if I give up candy and soda for a year?"

Melanie, with a slight grin and confidence that he couldn't do it, replied, "Five hundred dollars! Half goes in the bank or we invest it, and you can spend the other half however you want. And you will also feel a lot better!"

And that was all it took.

I'm not sure he did it for the "health" reasons or the "money" reasons, but it really doesn't matter. He did it. ONE straight year without ANY candy or soda.

And I'm so proud of him.

To think about the sacrifice, discipline, and WILLPOWER it took to accomplish that is impressive. Heck, to do anything for a year straight is impressive.

Or to NOT do something for a year is impressive.

Maybe it's caffeine. Or nicotine. Or alcohol. Or fast food. Or TV.

Hey, I'm not saying chocolate or coffee is bad in moderation. Or a glass of wine a week is bad for you.

But sometimes you just want to see if you can make a serious commitment and accomplish it. Or you may want to strengthen your WILLPOWER, so you put it to the test, giving it a workout, so to speak.

 **ACTION STEP**

Is there any habit in your life that you would like to see if you could give up or eliminate? Maybe it's for one week. Maybe a month or three months. Or maybe even a full year.

Search your heart. Put something on it. And then do it.

Thanks, Luke. You showed great resolve and mental toughness in not giving in when you really wanted to. You really bulked up your WILLPOWER muscle!

Now take that $250 and go invest it!

Much love. Much sacrifice. And much less "candy."

WOW 40
WAGGIN' TAILS

They say a dog is man's best friend. I think they're right. I remember my old Golden Retriever Sid when he was 13 and 14 years old. He was "old." I had to carry him up the steps at night because his legs would give out. His hearing was about done. He didn't move around very well anymore.

But he still wagged his tail when I would walk in the door at night.

He would wag his tail when we pet him, when we scratched his belly, and when we fed him. Basically, he would wag his tail whenever we paid attention to him and gave him some love. He was happy!

I sometimes say to my athletes and clients even now, "Wag your tail today." I got this from a strength and conditioning coach friend of mine, Kevin Reaume, who used to use it with his athletes at La Jolla Country Day School. I use it now too. And I like it.

So, what does it mean to wag your tail?

Waggin' your tail can mean you have "swagger." I think all athletes need swagger. I'm not saying to be a braggart or to be cocky. I'm simply saying to walk tall, walk confidently, and wag your tail. Body language must ooze confidence all the time.

Waggin' your tail can mean that you might need to "fake it till you feel it." I know there are days when you don't feel your best. Maybe you're facing challenge or adversity. Maybe there's an "energy vampire" in your life. You're beat-up, defeated, and downtrodden. I get it. It happens. But it doesn't mean you have to live in that world. Fill your mind with positivity and tell yourself to walk tall. Don't ever stop "waggin' your tail." I promise you, the simple act of waggin' it can get your mood going in the right direction. So wag it, baby, wag it!

Waggin' your tail means you're happy. It's important that we all shine in our lives. And we can best shine when we appreciate the small things in life. A friendly greeting. A warm touch. A good meal. Connecting with someone you love.

The message today is simple: **WAG YOUR TAIL**. And then tell your friends, colleagues, co-workers, clients, patients, children, and family to do the same. It puts a smile on your face and one on everyone around you. Say to them when leaving, "Hey, don't forget, **WAG YOUR TAIL** today." Watch the smile!

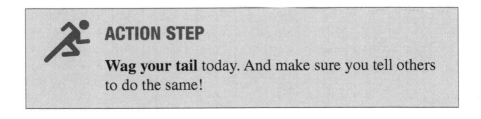

ACTION STEP

Wag your tail today. And make sure you tell others to do the same!

Sid eventually passed at the age of 15, and I was blessed to have him that long. And one thing he taught us up until the day he died was that regardless of how hard, how difficult, or how challenging a day may be, nothing is better than coming home to a **WAGGIN' TAIL**.

Time to **WAG IT**!

WOW 41

HUSTLE

Win one for the Gipper. David vs. Goliath. Shock the world.

I've used them all.

A few years ago, when my middle son Brady was just eight, I coached his rec soccer team. And we weren't very good. I always said, "We might not be the best soccer team, but I can promise you that 'Team IMPACT' WILL be the best-conditioned team on the field." ☺

Well, going into our final tournament of the season (that all teams make), we were the whopping number eight seed out of twelve teams.

In the first game against the number nine seed, we were down 1 0 at half. I used the ole "Win one for the Gipper" speech, and it worked like a gem. We won 2–1 and advanced to the next round.

In the second game of the day against the number two seed, we were down 2–0 at the half. After a "David vs. Goliath" speech at halftime, we miraculously came back and somehow won 5–3.

Despite heavy, tired legs, in the third game against the number five seed, we were tied 0–0 at the half.

And we were tied 2–2 at the end of regulation. Wow.

Time for penalty kicks. And at the end of five penalty kicks, we were still tied.

171

So we went into sudden death penalty kicks.

And on the seventh kick, Team IMPACT shocked the world (well, at least us, parents), and we WON.

The team went bananas. Dogpiled on each other. And it was absolute pandemonium.

We advanced to the finals. And this time it was against the top team in the league.

So in the fourth game of the day and coming off an emotional high, we had to immediately head to the FINALS with no rest, exhilarated and excited, but also exhausted.

I knew these little kids didn't have much in the tank, and I knew the other team was "only" playing their third game of the day.

So I had to employ every tactic in the book. I had already used "Win one for the Gipper." Already used "David vs. Goliath." And "Shock the world."

After introducing them to taking a few deep breaths, all I talked about was **HUSTLE**. That whether we won or lost in the finals, I just wanted to see them compete. And fight. And show heart. And show **HUSTLE**.

We lost the game. As a matter of fact, we got smoked about 7–1. I stopped counting when the clinic the other team was putting on scored the first five goals.

And I couldn't stop thinking about how darned proud I was to see my tired little boys out there **HUSTLING**. Competing. Playing hard. And even getting a goal in the second half.

When at halftime one of my kids asked, "Do we get second place ribbons?" I was reminded that I was coaching 8, 9, and 10 year olds. And I just smiled. And said yes.

It was a memorable experience. One of true IMPACT for those kids. I don't think they will ever forget the exhilaration of winning in penalty kicks. Or finishing second in the league after a year that was marked by mediocre outcomes . . . but also slow and steady improvement.

Sometimes you are dead-dog tired and can't muster up any more energy to do what you need to do. But that's when you have to find the strength and **HUSTLE** to find a way to get the job done.

ACTION STEP

Where in your life are you doing a good job **hustling**?

Are there any areas of your life that you feel you can do a better job hustling to get the results you want to get in your life?

Whether you are 8 years old or 80 years old, you gotta keep **HUSTLING** in life.

When you do, great things happen. And even if your "season" starts slow or it's just trudging along, just keep **HUSTLING**—great things will happen.

Thanks, Team IMPACT, for teaching me a life lesson. You gotta dig down deep when you're tired. And when all the motivational talks are done, just keep **HUSTLING**!

—Coach Todd

WOW 42

#42!!!

 Jackie Robinson was one of the best baseball players of ALL TIME. And in 1940, he broke out of the Negro Baseball League and made the Brooklyn Dodgers.

Now realize this   that was a very tumultuous time for a black athlete to be stepping into a league that was all white.

His life was in jeopardy, people wanted to kill him and his first-born son, they wouldn't let him sleep in the team hotels, opposing managers and fans would jeer him. Heck, even a few of his own teammates didn't agree with having a black player on the team and in that league.

Now think about that—What if that were you?

How scared would you be?

How scared do you think he was?

How much **COURAGE** do you think it took him to show up day in, day out, receiving hate mail, threats, and constant criticism?

Do you think he sometimes feared for his life?

Number 42 changed the game. Jackie Robinson had amazing **COURAGE** and **BRAVERY**. He was **persistent**. And he always took the "high road" when in the face of confrontation. And he was a superstar athlete. One of the very best.

How about you?

What are you scared of today? Where is FEAR holding you back from being your best? From changing the game? From being a pioneer or a trailblazer?

You see, everyone has fear. Fear of success or fear of failure. The bottom line is this—you never let FEAR stop you from being your best. **Let FEAR motivate you**. Let FEAR catapult and propel you to be a pioneer.

Let's be more like 42. A trailblazer. A pioneer. A leader. A winner.

ACTION STEP

What do you FEAR the most right now in your life?

And what can you do to use **FEAR** to **MOTIVATE** you and not paralyze you?

One of my clients and latest mentors, Pastor David Jeremiah of Turning Point Church (featured in WOW 50), once said something extremely powerful about FEAR to me, "If what you are doing doesn't scare you, then you are not dreaming big enough and walking by enough faith."

Now that is powerful.

Thank you, Jackie Robinson, for teaching us to stand up for what we believe in, despite objection, ridicule, mocking, hazing, and everything you had to endure to change the times.

Now, it's time to be like #42! Let's get going!

WOW 43
TRADITIONS WITH DAD

One of my favorite traditions when I was a boy was spending time with my dad in our local Hallmark card store on his birthday. I can vividly remember between the ages of 10 to 15, going to the Hallmark store and reading every birthday card made for dads. Because I didn't have money to buy the cards, we would just read them together and pick out ones that made us laugh. My memories of those 15 or 20 minutes we spent together in the card store each year still fill me with love and gratitude.

My dad died of a heart attack when I was 20 years old, and he has been gone for over 20 years now (Feb 19, 1992), but I still think about that birthday tradition every February 6. And on that date, I still always go over to the local card shop and spend about 20 minutes just perusing through the "Dad Birthday" cards. Just like WE used to do. Twenty minutes of smiling, laughing, and remembering.

Sometimes the simplest traditions are the most meaningful. Card "shopping" with my dad didn't cost a dime, but it was a great celebration of his birthday. We shared TIME together. And it became our tradition.

TIME. It's the most precious commodity each of us has to share with another. How is it that we get a fresh supply of it every day, yet we never seem to have enough? I know what you're thinking: "I'm always so busy." Heck, I'm right there with you. But every Feb 6 (albeit even for a few minutes), I put a lid on my "crazy busy" typical day and take a trip to the card store in honor of my dad and our birthday tradition from so many years ago.

And I NEVER regret that time. It always puts a smile on my face and a tear in my eye.

Sometimes we get so caught up in all that we have to do. Our to-do list seems to go on forever, but with all the hustle and bustle of work and family life, we really are at risk of "missing the forest for the trees." We have great intentions to spend quality time with loved ones. We dream about family vacations, romantic getaways, total relaxation, "mellow-yellow" time—call it what you will—but does it happen enough? Are you making memories? Are you creating traditions?

My friend, nothing is as valuable as the gift of your **TIME**.

After most of my visits to the card store on Feb 6, I go home and break open the folder of all Dad's handwritten letters he wrote to me when I was in college.

Can you imagine?—I received a handwritten letter from my dad EVERY SINGLE DAY while I was at William & Mary. Twenty-four years later, they still IMPACT me greatly.

So here's my message for you: don't wait for a birthday or a holiday to start an awesome tradition with someone you love. Ask yourself, "What can I do to create a tradition that will **IMPACT** someone I love today . . . and maybe for generations?"

- Handwrite a letter to your spouse or your child.

- Write a love letter to that special someone . . . just like you used to do.

- Start calling or texting once a day just to say hi or I love you.

- Surprise an older parent with an entire day of your time. Offer to do anything they need or want: cooking, cleaning, gardening, home repairs, lunch and a movie, a walk on the beach, shopping, etc.

- Book a vacation—anywhere, any length, anytime.

- Videotape an interview-style gratitude journal at your next family gathering. Upload it to YouTube with an "unlisted" video link just for family and friends.

- Call your best friend and play hooky for a day.

- Go to baseball spring training in Arizona or Florida.

- Interview a grandparent or older parent, and take notes. Show your interest in their early memories and beloved stories.

- Pay the day rate at the nicest hotel in your town, get in a great workout, and lounge around the pool and spa for a whole day.

- Start a game night or movie night tradition in your home.

- Stop wondering if you would enjoy camping, and find out. Borrow equipment for your first outing and have an adventure.

- Really get crazy and pick a night when "kids make the rules." Be ready for ice cream for dinner and sleeping in a tent in the backyard or family room . . .

- Video each member of your family telling a bedtime story or recalling their favorite memory.

- Plan a regular mother/son or father/daughter outing. Reverse it up next time.

- Go online to one of the photo sites (shutterfly.com, costcophotocenter.com, etc.) and create a "Why I Love You" or an "I Think You're Awesome" photo book for someone special.

- And, of course, visit your local card store on special occasions . . . just like my dad and me.

Traditions are what memories are built upon. They don't have to cost any money at all, but they do require some thoughtfulness, effort, and dedication. It's all about **TIME**, our most precious resource.

No matter if you can share 20 minutes, 20 hours, or 20 years, spend **time** with a loved one and start a new tradition. Get busy making memories that will keep you smiling, laughing, and remembering. They will fill you with love and gratitude. Two of my favorite things.

ACTION STEP

Choose ONE THING from above and take ACTION on creating that memory today!

WOW 44
GRATITUDE

There is nothing quite like the feeling of an "**ATTITUDE of GRATITUDE**."

As a matter of fact, if you are feeling stressed, anxious, or unhappy, spend MORE time in **GRATITUDE**.

By doing so, it really helps you feel better . . . and live better also.

After Hurricane Sandy ravaged my beloved Jersey Shore in 2012 (I grew up in Brick, New Jersey, on the Shore), my wife and I started the Durkin IMPACT Foundation. For years, I had always wanted to start a foundation but never got around to it.

Until this disaster struck.

I just had to do it . . . IMMEDIATELY!

Within three months, our fundraising efforts raised over $80,000. And we were able to donate 100% of that money directly to those directly affected by Sandy.

All in all, fifteen "big" checks went out to people in dire straits stemming from Hurricane Sandy.

And it felt really good to do that.

A few weeks later, I received two handwritten thank-you cards from recipients, expressing their heart-felt THANKS. And another person left an emotional voicemail expressing their THANKS. You could feel the emotion in their voice. And you could discern it in their writing.

It made me think about **GRATITUDE**. It made me think about appreciation. And it made me think about the power of a handwritten thank-you card and voicemail.

The WOW is **GRATITUDE**.

You don't need to start a foundation to have **GRATITUDE**. But you can give of your time, energy, or money to philanthropic efforts that align with your passion.

One of my best practices now is keeping a gratitude journal. Several days a week for five to ten minutes, I write what I'm grateful for in my journal.

For example, here is a recent journal entry I did on **GRATITUDE**.

GRATITUDE

1. *Melanie*. Her health, love, and support. She really is my biggest cheerleader and support.

2. *My kids*. Luke, Brady, and McKenna are all unique and special in their own right. Continue to bless them with encouragement, praise, and love.

3. *My mother*. She's 82 years old now. There is not a single phone conversation that goes by that I don't just cherish. I am grateful for her voice and love.

4. *My extended family*. My 7 brothers and sisters. Stephen, Paul, Patti, Pam, Mary Beth, Judy, and Karen. I love having 2 older brothers and 5 older sisters. And while I don't get to talk or see them as much as I want, I am grateful they are in my life. Please bless over their health and happiness.

5. *Fitness Quest 10.* Our entire team. All of our clients. The actual brick and mortar—our "sanctuary"—where we work to share our passion every day. That is a blessing, and I'm extremely grateful that I get to do what I love, every single day!

6. *My own health.* It is said, "He who has his health has a thousand dreams. He who does not, has one." I am so thankful that I have my health and that I feel vibrant, empowered, energized, and inspired to help transform people's lives.

7. *My Mastermind.* Man, I love my Mastermind. I love having the opportunity to coach hundreds of fitness pros on an on-going basis. They really do inspire me to do even more profound work. And I love seeing them do incredible work also.

8. *Speaking at various conferences and events worldwide.* Two of my passions are speaking and traveling. And because I get to combine them, it makes me full of even more passion. I never want to take for granted the one, two, hundred, thousand, or more people that might go to an event to hear me speak or present. I am honored and grateful whenever I have the opportunity to speak on the platform. #KeepTheFire

9. *The Durkin IMPACT Foundation.* Since starting our foundation in 2013, we have raised over $250,000 that has gone to great causes. Hurricane Sandy victims. We have given scholarships to 19 student-athletes that went on to college. I am grateful for this opportunity to give back and hope and pray that it will play an even bigger role in the future.

10. *My relationship with God.* My faith has always been important. Since I was young, God has always been in my life. I was raised Catholic and devoutly went to mass. Today, I practice as a "non-denominational" Christian. Here is a recent prayer and one that I often pray, "Lord, please be in my heart and in my head. Provide me the courage to continue

leading on all levels. And Lord, allow me to follow YOUR will, not mine. Whatever your path is for me, give me the strength, courage, and knowledge to follow your purpose for me so that I can, in turn, glorify you. Thank you. Amen."

There you have it. Ten things I am grateful for. I know it's quite personal. But after all, it is my journal entry.

And I encourage you to be real in yours also.

ACTION STEP

Take time today to journal in your WOW Journal or even start a gratitude journal. Maybe it's just ten minutes per night for the next week.

There is no right or wrong way.

You can bullet out who/what you are most grateful for or who/what you most appreciate. You can write it out in paragraphs.

The point is that you are actually taking conscious time to consciously express **GRATITUDE**. And that shifts your mindset and energy in really powerful ways.

GRATITUDE. It's your WOW.

WHY? Because we have so much to be GRATEFUL for. The little things. And the BIG things.

I have found that you don't want to wait until Thanksgiving to be grateful. It's better to live in an "**ATTITUDE of GRATITUDE**" right NOW and every day moving forward.

Much love . . . and much thanks!

WOW 45
CHANGE & YOUR BIG 5

There are four guarantees in life. Birth. Death. Taxes. And **CHANGE**.

And while most people don't love **CHANGE**, **CHANGE** is also inevitable. It's part of growth.

Maybe the **CHANGE** is small. Or maybe it's big.

Possibly it's physical. Or maybe mental/emotional. Spiritual. Relational. Professional/career.

Regardless, all **CHANGE** involves transition, and all transition involves **CHANGE**.

If there are things in your life that you keep saying over and over that you are going to do (lose weight, create a certain product/program, become an author or a speaker, take a special trip, do this, do that . . .), what are you waiting for?

Seriously, what are you waiting for?

At the same time, I know many people in times of transitions right now.

Transitions in the workplace.

Transitions in phases of life.

Transitions with family.

Transitions with relationships.

Transitions personally.

Realize that in times of transition, there are many uncertainties. And that can be scary.

But that's also life.

And it's also the beauty of LIVING. There is yin and yang. There is light and dark. There is sun and rain. There are peaks and valleys. There are highs and lows. And there is winning and losing. And without one, you can't appreciate the other. Ultimately, life's continued challenge is to embrace the new opportunities, possibilities for personal growth, and unexpected new adventures that **TRANSITIONS** and **CHANGE** provide.

Maybe it comes down to getting back to your best practices. Reading thirty-plus minutes a day on personal development, cleaning up your diet, including more cardio with your program, getting bodywork more regularly.

Or maybe it has to do directly with your profession or career.

CHANGE doesn't necessarily mean you need to quit your job and go elsewhere. Sometimes people think it takes extreme measures to **CHANGE**. Not always. The grass is not always greener on the other side of the fence.

Maybe it just requires more effort on your end to create the **CHANGE** you wish to see within your organization.

Maybe you can become the social media director within your brand. Or contribute to posting blogs.

Or run all online content.

Or manage the website.

Or maybe you want nothing to do with any of that.

Maybe you need to get outside the four walls of your facility or business to connect with more prospects and get more clients.

Or maybe you need to reach out more to existing customers to assist with client retention.

Or maybe you need to deliver more "and then some" customer service.

I learned this universal principle many years ago, "To get more, you must GIVE more. You must SERVE more."

All of it takes effort and **CHANGE**, but you must be intentional about your stated actions.

Ask yourself these two questions:

1. What 5 things do I want to accomplish in my lifetime?

2. What 5 things do I want to accomplish this year?

And are your current efforts and focus helping you achieve what you set out to do for the year and your life?

If so, stay focused and keep plowing forward.

If not, it's time to **CHANGE**.

ACTION STEP

Answer the two pressing questions that can help get or keep you on the right track to live out your purpose.

1. What 5 things do you want to accomplish this year?

2. What 5 things do you want to accomplish in your life?

Now start **CHANGING**!

WOW 46

DISNEY

"Dad, we like you better at Disney!"

Melanie and I took our three kids to Disneyland when they were 8, 6, and 3 for a summer vacation. Three days at the "happiest place on Earth"—well, at least that's what they say it is!

Disneyland really is an amazing adventure, filled with laughter, smiles, tons of rides (my personal favorites are Space Mountain and Thunder Mountain Railroad), and very happy children and parents. If you've visited an amusement park in the summer months, you know firsthand that each visit comes with plenty of time to hangout with family and friends (this is code for "standing in line"). I came home wiser for the experience and wanted to share some thoughts with you.

Call it a vision. Call it a BHAG (big, hairy, audacious goal). Call it what you want, but the story of how Walt Disney created his Magic Kingdom is amazing, and the magic he brought to millions of people worldwide is truly inspiring. I think there's a lesson here for all of us. I know there were one or two for me. First, I'll give you a little background.

Walt Disney's path to becoming an entertainment giant and international icon wasn't easy. And neither was the path to building Disneyland . . . but it is pretty interesting. Walt bought land amidst the strawberry farms in Anaheim despite much public rebuke. And when Disneyland opened on July 17, 1955, opening day was such a disaster, insiders later referred to it as Black Sunday.

A plumbing strike forced a choice between running toilets or drinking fountains. Walt chose properly functioning toilets over drinking fountains and then woke to scorching temperatures. His carefully planned, invitation-only event for 11,000 people quickly turned into 28,000 due to counterfeit tickets. Recently poured asphalt wasn't dry by opening, and women's heels sank into the streets and pathways. A gas leak forced the closure of Adventureland, Frontierland, and Fantasyland, making it impossible for guests to enjoy most of the park. In other words, opening day at Disneyland was less about magic and more about malfunction.

Walt was no stranger to adversity—filing for bankruptcy earlier in his career was just one bump in the road. But through it all, he remained true to his vision. What began with a disastrous start eventually became the Magic Kingdom we all know and love. Folks, Walt Disney created IMPACT.

So here I was at Disney, pondering the magic around me. How did he do it? How did he build something that has given such joy to so many millions for so many years? In other words, how could this man have created an environment so magical that people willingly wait in line for an hour or more just to enjoy a two-minute ride and then declare his creation, the *happiest place on Earth*?

It took no more than two young boys to show me how it was done. My sons, Luke and Brady, gave me the answer to my question, and I'd like to pass it along to you.

There I was on day two, standing in a long line with my boys who were dying to go on Splash Mountain. It was about a sixty-minute wait and would be our fifth ride of the day. Everyone's patience was wearing thin, so we agreed it was an excellent time for rock-paper-scissors. Many games later, we were ready for the BIG GAME. The winner would be the Grand-Pupa Rock-Paper-Scissors Champion of the World.

Just then, my eight-year old son, Luke, stops, looks at me, and says, "Dad, Brady and I have been talking . . . We like you better at Disneyland."

I laughed and thought, "What? My kids like me better at Disney. What's that supposed to mean?"

So I asked, "Huh . . . what do you mean by that? And what do you mean by 'we'? Is there some kind of conspiracy here?"

Luke explained, "Well, Dad, you've been playing ever since we got here. All the rides, the lines, tossing us in the swimming pool at the hotel . . . You've been a ton of fun. You haven't been on your phone. You're holding Mom's hand . . . We like you better at Disneyland!"

I immediately thought, "Man, am I not fun at home? Do I not play like this at work or home?"

Sadly, the answer was NO.

I knew the kind of play Luke was talking about—free-wheeling, no holds barred, all-out fun. I don't play like that at work or at home. The boys were right; I was more fun at Disneyland. I needed to **PLAY MORE**.

Right in front of me—there was the answer to my question. Walt Disney believed in **PLAY**. He actually designed and built Disneyland to be all about **PLAY**. Before Disneyland was built, he made movies, and the park was envisioned as a place where Walt's own employees could **play** with their children. It all came together for me . . . **PLAY** is the key to the Magic Kingdom.

Sure, we all know every day can't be vacation, a trip to Disneyland, or even a rock-paper-scissors championship. But Walt had it right.

Play fuels our work. It was his commitment to **play** that allowed him to achieve his life's work—to realize his vision.

We've got to **PLAY MORE**. **Play** to connect with those around us. **Play** to tap into our imagination. **Play** to express what's in our heart. And when we do, we'll find the magic just like Walt did.

I will never forget our rock-paper-scissors championship and how one simple comment from my kids could teach me such an important life lesson. It was the best part of my entire vacation, and I wanted to share it with you, my friends . . . Have a strong vision. **PLAY** with passion. LIVE with purpose. And create IMPACT every day!

ACTION STEP

What can you do to **PLAY** more today?

How can you be more present in your conversations, with your kids or spouse?

Can you book a trip that will allow for some quality time connecting with family?

Regardless, laugh, smile, have fun . . . and **PLAY** today. And oh yeah, throw in a game of rock-paper-scissors!

Thank you, Luke, and thank you, Brady, for reminding Daddy that I really am "better at Disneyland." And thank you, Walt Disney, for the IMPACT of a lasting memory.

WOW 47
220 IN A 110 WORLD

One of the most empowering and humbling things you can do is attend an event related to the military.

I've been to Marines Corps "Boot Camp" graduations.

I've been to Marine Corps "Promotion" ceremonies.

And I've been to multiple military retirement ceremonies.

And they are all awesome in their own right.

I recently attended one of my friend's retirement ceremonies from the US Marines Corps. Lt. Colonel Greg Bond was much decorated, and after twenty-eight years of service, it was time for him to retire his stripes.

At these very patriotic and inspiring ceremonies, the retiree also gets a guest speaker that comes in and talks about the new retiree's career. This one held at MCRD San Diego was no different.

Lt. Colonel Greg Bond had Major General Michael G. Dana (a two-star general) come in from the Pentagon and speak. These two very close friends had worked together and been on deployments together.

General Dana came in on a beautiful but very windy day and did something surprising. Whereas all the other speakers were using a microphone because of the blustery (loud) winds, General Dana walked away from the podium, saying that he would not be needing a microphone, stood in front of Greg, and in his raspy, loud drill-instructor voice, spoke about his friend, Lt. Colonel Greg Bond.

He spoke of Greg's service. He spoke about his honor, courage, and commitment to the Corps. He talked about his attitude and aptitude. He talked about his tireless work ethic. And he spoke about Greg as a person.

And then he said something special.

General Dana said, "Lt. Colonel Greg Bond is a 220 man operating in a 110 world."

Dang, that is awesome. A 220 man operating in a 110 world.

A 220 person in a 110 world. This means several things.

It means his energy is a step ahead of everyone else's.

That his productivity is superior to everyone else's.

That his attitude is extremely positive, despite his not always being in the best of circumstances or locations.

And General Dana gave examples of all these from when he was on deployments with Lt. Colonel Bond in Guam, Korea, the Philippines, Hawaii, and a few other places.

He said it's no mistake why Greg leads greatly so many men.

That it's no mistake why people love spending time with him.

That it's no mistake why he is respected by so many.

That it's no mistake that he's had such a successful career in the Marines.

Because of his 220 attitude.

220 is 2 x 110. Twice as good. No time to be average. It's about a higher level of productivity. Intensity. Focus. Positivity. Just a bit above the norm!

So bring the heat today . . . and then some!

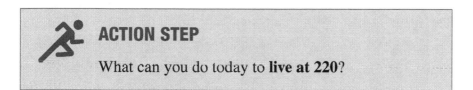

ACTION STEP

What can you do today to **live at 220**?

Now go light it up!

WOW 48
TOUCH

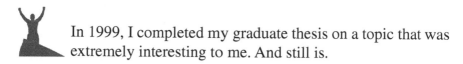 In 1999, I completed my graduate thesis on a topic that was extremely interesting to me. And still is.

My two-year research project at San Diego State University was entitled "The Physiological and Psychological Effects of Massage Therapy on Stress and Anxiety."

I actually have an extensive massage therapy and bodywork background. It's part of my story. It's part of my training. It's part of who I am.

And it's bodywork (specifically Rolfing/structural work) that also got me out of pain and off nine months of needing Vicodin every day (you can read more about that story in my *IMPACT* book). But that's not specifically the purpose of today's message.

The purpose of today's message is to talk about the POWER OF **TOUCH**.

When writing my master's thesis, I cited Dr. Tiffany Field, at the **Touch** Research Institute in Miami, Florida, talking about how infants that are coddled and touched grow physically and psychologically at a much more rapid rate. Additionally she discussed the importance and power of **touch** amongst seniors. Quite fascinating stuff.

Touch can represent many things. It can represent compassion. Care. Empathy. Love.

And under the skilled hands of a manual therapist (massage therapist, bodyworker, chiropractor, or physical therapist), it can mean additional things:

- Relief from pain

- Improved mobility and flexibility

- Improved recovery

- Relaxation

- Or just pure bliss

You see, whenever you receive an exceptional therapeutic massage, you FEEL BETTER. And when you feel better, you are a better husband or wife. A better son or daughter. A better boss. A better employee. Just a better human being. Because you FEEL BETTER. This is a good thing.

But why is it that people often wait until something is wrong to "fix" the pain? Or to get rid of that bottled up stress?

Like a squirrel storing nuts for a long winter, many people often don't take advantage of the regular benefits of therapeutic massage until they are already in pain. Or until their body doesn't feel good. Or until they are extremely stressed out.

Just like I found statistical differences on stress and anxiety due to massage (the physical parameters measured were blood pressure, heart rate, and respiration rate; the psychological parameter was a "State Trait Anxiety Inventory," a survey measuring state of mind before/after a fifteen-minute seated massage) in my study many years ago, massage has been proven to decrease blood pressure, heart rate, and respiration rate. And these benefits can be traced back hundreds, if not thousands, of years.

The idea is that therapeutic massage and bodywork serve as

preventative tools to the deleterious side effects of stress, anxiety, the daily pressures of life, over-training, etc.

I still remember at an IDEA World Fitness conference in July 2007, fitness industry icon Augie Nieto was on stage sharing a few precious words. Augie was the creator and CEO of Life Fitness equipment. He contracted ALS or Lou Gehrig's disease in March 2005. And he's been courageously fighting it ever since.

And on that July morning in 2007 in a wheelchair up on stage with Peter and Kathie Davis, he made a comment that I will never forget.

Augie said, "If you see me at this conference . . . please, please . . . come **TOUCH ME**."

"Please come **TOUCH** me."

While it took him about three minutes to articulate this sentence, it was clear as day what Augie wanted.

He wanted to be touched. He wanted compassion. He wanted a pat on the back, a handshake, or a hug. Ultimately, he wanted love. He wanted **TOUCH**.

Augie continues to fight the good fight today, battling this disease admirably. And his foundation has raised millions of dollars to help fight ALS. I'm sure touch continues to play a role in Augie's fight.

My friends, whether it's a friendly handshake, a pat on the back, a hug, or a professional therapeutic massage session encapsulating skilled touch, let's be aware of touch and the important role it plays in every day of our lives.

And whether it's an infant being coddled, the last days of your life, or somewhere in between, know that **TOUCH** plays a significant role in your overall health of body, mind, and spirit.

Remember the power of touch this week in all you do. You don't have to be a massage therapist or on your deathbed to positively "touch" someone this week.

🏃 ACTION STEP

Do something today to **TOUCH** someone positively in your life.

Maybe it's going out of your way to **"touch"** a stranger by performing a great deed or providing a warm handshake or gentle pat on the shoulder.

Or maybe it's someone that you are close to in your life every day that you often overlook or take for granted. Give them a caring and loving hug. An encouraging smile. Or give your spouse or loved one an "in-home" massage.

Or maybe you can receive a "professional" massage yourself or receive some much-needed bodywork from the hands of a skilled therapist.

Heck, maybe it's just a friendly **"touch"** of encouragement and voice of acknowledgement and support.

What's it going to be?

Write it down, commit to it, and get it done.

What can you commit to? Do something today that includes the POWER OF **TOUCH**.

Until next time, keep learning . . . keep loving . . . and keep "touching."

Much love . . . and much **TOUCH**.

WOW 49
SINK OR SWIM?

Do you like to be "tested"?

For some, a test conjures up images of biology, chemistry, or economics exams back in high school or college.

For others, a test may mean something physical, such as a "fitness test" or a "PT test."

And yet for others, it could be the "test of a lifetime."

In January 2015, I heard an incredible story that just blew my mind. It involved former NFL fullback and Syracuse football standout, Rob Konrad, who certainly had the TEST of a lifetime.

It was also a TEST of sheer willpower . . . and some luck was involved also!

Konrad had been out fishing in the Atlantic Ocean off the coast of South Florida. And as he hooked a fish, with his boat on auto-drive at five mph, a wave hit the boat and threw Konrad into the ocean. And he happened to be all by himself.

His boat continued to drive away as he was left alone in the ocean about nine miles out. No life preserver. No phone. Nothing.

So Konrad began to **SWIM**. With strong currents and choppy waves, he did his best to **SWIM** towards shore. But many times, he was going the wrong way because of the currents.

He had no water.

Here are a few things that happened over the course of the sixteen-hour ordeal:

A shark came and circled him a few times . . . And then it left.

A boat came within a hundred yards of him . . . And did not see him.

A search and rescue helicopter flew practically over top of him . . . And it did not see him.

How disheartening would that be? And how scary would that be also?

After sixteen hours at sea and **SWIMMING** approximately twenty-seven miles because of the strong currents, he miraculously made it onto shore . . . and survived!

What allowed him to do that?

Was it pure adrenaline?

Survival instinct?

A burning desire to continue living for his wife and kids?

His FAITH in God?

What was it that allowed him to survive?

To me, that IS a test. An absolutely HUGE test.

I've thought several times—*What would I do if I were in that situation?*

What would I do if a shark were circling me?

What would I do if I were **SWIMMING** for survival out in the middle of the ocean?

What would I do if I had hypothermia and was extremely dehydrated?

How about you—What would you do? **SINK** or **SWIM**?

My hope is WE would do what Rob Konrad did—keep **SWIMMING**, floating, treading, and moving inch by inch towards shore. And **NEVER GIVE UP**. Never **SINK**.

Hey, we've all been **TESTED** in some way. Some harder than others. But we've all been **TESTED**.

Maybe you are going through a TEST now. Or maybe you're going to have a big, unexpected TEST coming up.

A coach once imparted sage wisdom in regards to competing and testing: "Expect the best. Prepare for the worst."

The bottom line is that we do our best to keep preparing for our tests in life.

Perhaps you have been "tested" recently, or you are going through a test now . . .

Maybe it's your primary relationship that is being tested.

Or you have several "tests" going on at work.

Or perhaps you have some physical challenges going on.

Today, I want you to TEST yourself physically. I want you to get in a GREAT workout. And do that for at least thirty minutes.

 (If you need some ideas or specific challenges, hop over to the website url below where I have posted five demanding, "IMPACT-inspired" workout challenges for you to TEST yourself.)

Whether by choice, accident, or fate—think about how and when you can TEST yourself this week to a level previously not attempted. Challenge yourself to **SINK** or **SWIM**. What's it going to be?

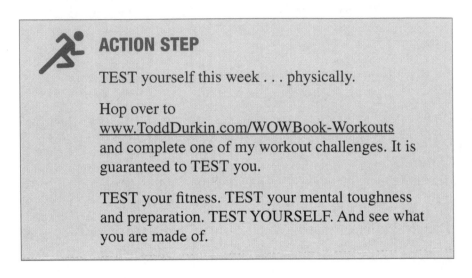

ACTION STEP

TEST yourself this week . . . physically.

Hop over to www.ToddDurkin.com/WOWBook-Workouts and complete one of my workout challenges. It is guaranteed to TEST you.

TEST your fitness. TEST your mental toughness and preparation. TEST YOURSELF. And see what you are made of.

And by the way, if an unexpected TEST comes up in any area of your life, what are you going to do—**SINK** or **SWIM**?

Thanks, Rob Konrad, for showing us what to do!

WOW 50
"DR. J" & COMMITMENT

"It was character that got us out of bed, COMMITMENT that moved us into ACTION, and discipline that enabled us to follow through.
—Zig Ziglar

Pastor David Jeremiah has been a client of mine for a few years now. He comes in three times a week in the middle of the day for his physical training and conditioning, and flexibility, energy, and mindset surge.

Pastor Jeremiah, or "Dr. J," as I like to call him because he once was a basketball star back at Cedarville High School in Cedarville, Iowa, and then Cedarville College, is also one of the busiest men I know.

Dr. Jeremiah is the senior pastor of Shadow Mountain Church in San Diego and annually disciples millions of people worldwide on his nationally syndicated radio and television ministry, Turning Point (www.DavidJeremiah.org). He certainly is a man of **IMPACT**.

He also epitomizes **discipline** and **COMMITMENT**.

Pastor Jeremiah is 75 years old. And he trains like he is preparing for the NFL. He trains hard, and he always **challenges** himself to be his **best**. He has **tenacious spirit** and the **will of a warrior**.

He does the bench press. He pushes prowlers. Pulls sleds. Rows with the TRX. Swings kettlebells. Uses the battling ropes. He boxes. Does speed and agility work. And he dribbles a basketball quite well—still.

Pastor Jeremiah never misses a scheduled training session if he's in town. Ever.

Why does he train so **intensely**, with such **consistency** and the **mindset** and **COMMITMENT** of a **champion**?

Because he knows the importance of his physical health, energy, and vitality, and how it affects his life and his preaching. He understands the strong connection between the mind, body, and spirit. He often talks about training from the "inside out."

It's one thing to intellectually understand the benefits of training and exercise and another thing to **intentionally** schedule it in—in the middle of your day at the most inconvenient time—and do it over and over again without fail. And never miss! Now that is **discipline** and **COMMITMENT**.

And that is Pastor Jeremiah.

When I originally asked Dr. J why he didn't want to train in the early morning or after his workday, he explained, "If this training thing is going to be important to me, I need to prioritize it and put it smack in the middle of my day to prove that I can do it and will do it."

Pastor Jeremiah went on to say, "If you truly want to see the priorities of a person, simply look at their calendar and it will tell all. Additionally, I believe the same muscle that is needed to study and read Scripture each morning is the same muscle that is needed to work out and exercise. And that muscle is called **discipline** and **COMMITMENT**. When you look at my calendar and schedule, you'll know that I prioritize my health and exercise as much as my spiritual walk and journey."

My response—"WOW!!!"

If that doesn't fire you up, nothing will.

Most people say they don't have enough time in a day to do what they want. However, Pastor Jeremiah reinforces that we all have the same amount of time in a day. And how we choose to spend our time, who we choose to spend it with, and what time we spend actually doing it will all contribute to our ultimate success and happiness.

ACTION STEP

How can you exhibit more **discipline** and **COMMITMENT** in your life?

What practices can you rearrange or reestablish to make sure your body, mind, and soul are prioritized properly?

Here are a few ideas:

- Maybe you want to establish your "holy hour" at 5:30 am and get in time to read Scripture or simply to pray.

- Maybe you want to commit to 30 minutes of exercise per day, 5 days a week. And maybe it's first thing in the morning or after your day is done. Or perhaps you want to do it smack in the middle of your day—just like Dr. J.

- Maybe you want to hire a coach or trainer to motivate you, guide you, and hold you accountable for your actions.

- Maybe you want to prioritize your nutrition and stop drinking sodas, reduce all the sugars (breads, pasta, and alcohol count here!) and refined foods in your diet, and indulge in desserts only 2 days a week instead of five.

- Or maybe you want to improve your nutrition by adding a few things—a greens shake in the morning, more fruits and vegetables throughout the day, more lean protein (chicken and fish), a protein shake, and more water (half your body weight in fluid ounces).

- Maybe it's reading one book a month during your lunch break or before going to bed.

- Maybe it's career-related, and you need to attain an additional certification or degree to help you get to where you want to go.

- Perhaps it's in your relationships, and you need to establish a weekly "date night" again with your spouse. Or "special time" with your kids.

COMMIT today to being the best version of yourself. Write down what you are **COMMITTING** to and how you are going to do it. And then share it with a "significant other" in your life.

CHOOSE the **discipline** needed to do what you need to do on a **daily** basis.

And then do it.

Take ACTION on what it is that you want in life—over and over again!

Thank you, Pastor Jeremiah, for being a great example of how to live life in balance. You have taught me a lot of lessons about life in our years of training together—none more important than the value of **COMMITMENT** and **discipline** if we want something bad enough. You are a **true champion**!

> Go to
> www.ToddDurkin.com/WOWBook-PastorJeremiah
> to hear an exclusive interview with Dr. Jeremiah
> and me from Fitness Quest 10 after one of his
> training sessions. You will even see "Dr. J" getting
> after it in one of his workouts.

WOW 51
STRENGTH

Strength. We all need it. Sometimes more than others.

Physical **strength**. Mental **strength**. Emotional **strength**. Spiritual **strength**.

Where do you need the most **STRENGTH** right now? What requires the most attention? What is weakest right now?

Let me take you back to a WOW journal entry of mine from July 10, 2012 as it's a powerful one:

Most of you know the last few weeks have been very rough with the passing of longtime friends and clients Ken Sawyer and Louie Barajas. In many ways, I feel I have been walking around in a fog. The IDEA World Fitness show this past weekend was a great "distraction" and immersion into a ton of positive energy. It felt great to be around a ton of fitness pro colleagues. A special shout-out to the many FQ10 team members, our interns, and the many Mastermind members that were present at IDEA and who assisted me with classes. Thank you. I needed that.

On the drive home this morning, I had many mixed emotions. Ten days of intense grieving and then going ALL OUT at IDEA. I had a sense of relief, pride, and exhaustion—all at the same time. The plan was to attend my son Luke's soccer game at noon and then completely chill for the rest of the day. And that was to include a big-fat nap.

But plans changed.

Luke broke his arm today in his soccer game, and we spent the better part of the day in the emergency room. And you know it takes a lot of **STRENGTH** just to get through that. Luke was the goalie, and he got kicked diving for a ball. He ended up breaking his radius and ulna, and had to have them reset. He's in a cast up to his shoulder and will be in that for about five to eight weeks. Bummer.

There are two ways to look at this:

1. "When it rains it pours" or "Things happen in threes, and this is the third."

— OR —

2. PERSPECTIVE. In the big picture, a broken arm is not "bad" when you compare it to a situation like Sawman's (getting hit by a car and dying at age 51) or Louie's (dying of stomach cancer at age 58). It's a broken arm. It stinks. It ruins some summer plans for the kid.

When we got home from the ER, I asked Luke what were 2 or 3 of the things that this experience could teach him that might end up being positive. And the first thing he said was that he would have the opportunity to "work on my left." Good perspective.

It's not going to be an easy 5 to 8 weeks for him. But he's going to be OK. I told him I'd get him on a great supplement routine, he can work on his nutrition, and he can catch up on his rest (he can't swim, sweat, or get the arm wet).

STRENGTH. We all need it.

My **STRENGTH** is going to come in many forms this week and the upcoming next few weeks. I WILL:

- *Get good, quality sleep this week.* Four to five hours per night last week doesn't work. Grieving. Eulogies. Support.

- *Praying.* I need to make sure I remain mentally and spiritually strong, despite being emotionally tired. Praying and resting will revitalize this.

- *Time off.* Our scheduled family vacation isn't until August. But I WILL build in some "mellow-yellow" time before then.

- *Continue to TRAIN hard.*

- *Get a ninety-minute massage this week.*

- *Be present for Luke.*

The WOW is **STRENGTH**. We all face adversity. We all have different things in our lives. Personal. Business. Family. I get it.

And sometimes it does pour when it rains. Be prepared for that. God will never give you more than you can handle.

Think about what you are going to do today to muster up the **STRENGTH** you need. It's all about perspective and making sure we CHOOSE to tackle this stuff head-on.

ACTION STEP

What are you going to do to be **STRONG** today? Physically. Mentally. Emotionally. And spiritually.

Make sure you stay **STRONG** this week. And count the blessings you DO have . . . not the ones you DON'T have.

It's all about perspective . . . and staying **STRONG**! #BeSTRONG

WOW 52

FOOTBALL, PEANUTS & CRACKER JACKS

There I was, sitting in the Rose Bowl in Pasadena, California, amongst 94,402 rabid fans at the college national championship football game in January 2014 between Florida State University and Auburn University.

And I was loving being there with my two sons. As I looked to my left, I saw my 11-year-old son, Luke, intently watching the game. And as I looked to my right, I saw my 8-year-old son, Brady, intently eating peanuts and Cracker Jacks, and staring up at the Goodyear Blimp.

And then I looked out onto the field and saw two incredible teams— the Auburn Tigers and the Florida State Seminoles battling it out intensely. Determined to leave it all on the field.

It was then that I thought to myself, "Wow! Football and life. They just go together. Like fathers and sons. Like peanuts and Cracker Jacks."

Let's go deep on a "9 route" and take this opportunity to point out 13 ways that *football is like life*. There's something here for everyone.

1. **It takes 11 guys working together to accomplish the goal.**
    And the goal for the offense is to work together to progress the ball past the goal line for 6 points. The job for the 11 guys

on defense is to stop the guys who are trying to strategically advance the ball down the field.

Regardless of your industry, organization, or profession, it always takes a team of people working together to produce extraordinary results. Communication, clarity of roles, feedback, and support are all vital to the success of a team.

2. **Strategy counts.** Like anything in life, when you have a good strategy, you put yourself in a situation to win. If you just show up and play, chances are your team is not going to do well. In this way, football, business, and life are all the same.

3. **Preparation is the key to success.** In football, the more you watch film, study opponents, improve your technique, master your assignments, and know the plan, the better your chances for winning. I like the saying, "Failing to plan is planning to fail." Planning and preparation win the day.

    Perhaps the best story I can tell on this subject occurred a few years ago. I took my family down to New Orleans to see my long-time client, Drew Brees, play against the Chicago Bears. Drew invited us to come over to the team facility when we arrived late on Friday afternoon, so he could show the kids around.

    When we pulled into the Saints facility at about 5 pm on a Friday, two days before the Sunday game, there were only two or three cars in the entire parking lot. One of them was Drew's. He was at the facility late studying film, reviewing the playbook, and making final preparations. Everyone else was gone. Drew was studying. It's these little things that count. Remember, "There is never a traffic jam along the extra mile."

4. **Maximize your talent and potential**. It doesn't matter if it's football, teaching, coaching, business, or school. Man,

you have to maximize your God-given talents. Physically and mentally. Maximizing involves extraordinary sacrifice. It involves tremendous discipline. It requires belief and hard work. And then some.

5. **Physical conditioning is paramount to creating greatness**. Success in football requires you to be strong, fast, quick, powerful, flexible, and coordinated. Pro athletes need to be dialed into their nutrition, supplementation, massage/bodywork, sleep, and use of other recovery strategies.

   It's no different in life. If you want to be great in your career, you have to be in the best shape of your life. You need to train with the same discipline and work ethic as a pro athlete. I'm not saying you need to jump onto 40-inch boxes, bench press 300 pounds, or squat 500 pounds. But I am saying you need to devote 45 to 60 focused minutes per day on fitness, 6 times per week, to be your absolute best—in the boardroom, in your business, in your relationships, and in your homelife.

6. **Gotta have some thoroughbreds on your team**. Hey, let's face it—you need some talent on your team to excel. As motivational speaker Dave Ramsey once commented, "Thoroughbreds like hanging out with other thoroughbreds. They don't like hanging out with donkeys." I love that!

   But you don't need a bunch of superstars or renegades. You just need a few game changers who can elevate an organization. And you hope like the dickens they fit within the chemistry of the club.

7. **Leadership at all levels**. OK, I'll admit it. I am NOT a huge New England Patriots fan. Not sure why, I'm just not. But interesting enough, I am a huge fan of head coach Bill Belichick. This guy amazes me. He might be one of the best football coaches of all time.

Besides his sheer number of wins, I'm amazed how he takes guys who are misfits from all over the league, brings them into his system and culture, and helps them PRO-duce. Belichick has had some real characters on that team, but you don't hear a lot of negative press about his athletes (other than Aaron Hernandez).

As a matter of fact, besides Tom Brady and "The Gronk," the average football fan in America (outside the Boston/New England area) would be hard pressed to identify many other starters for this team.

WHY?

Leadership. This is the genius of the culture Belichick has created.

Leadership, leadership, leadership. If you want to be great in life or business, you need to be surrounded by great leadership. And you need to be a great leader yourself.

8. **You need a great "team" of people around you**. In football, if you're the head coach, you need great assistant coaches. You need a great supporting cast of administrators (owner, GM, player personnel, scouts). You need great strength coaches. You need a great medical team. You need many "good" players who are coachable and ready to be made "great."

   In life, who is the team around you? Do you have a coach? Do you train with a trainer? Who is your accountant? Who is your attorney? Who is your financial advisor? Who is your pastor? Who are the five people closest to you? All of these people count when it comes to maximizing success in life.

   What you typically find is that most every successful athlete or executive has mentors and/or coaches who have helped them attain success in life. Who is on your team?

Surround yourself with people who empower you, who teach you, and who motivate and inspire you to be your best.

9. **Be ready to call an audible**. In football, you see the quarterbacks checking and changing plays at the line of scrimmage all the time. This is called an audible. And it's because they want to run a different play (than the planned one) against the defense they see or anticipate.

   In life, sometimes we need to call an audible. Sometimes things just aren't going the way we intend. That doesn't mean you should stop trying or give up (heck, you never want to "quit" anything mid-season), but sometimes you just have to go in a different direction. So if you feel like you keep banging your head against the same drum over and over again and the tune is not right, maybe it's time to call an audible and go in a different direction.

10. **Overcome adversity**. Every team faces adversity. Some big. Some small. But in every game and every season, every team will face some setbacks. And it's how you respond to that adversity that counts.

    How about in your life? Facing any challenges? Feel like you're losing the battle? Stressed or anxious? Facing financial difficulties? Is there a relationship that's not going the way you hoped? So go into halftime, regroup, take a few deep breaths, create a new strategy that can get you out of the mess you are in, and then EXECUTE.

11. **Eliminate mental errors and mistakes**. Turnovers will kill a football team. So will dumb penalties (e.g., unsportsmanlike conduct). So will blown assignments. It takes great focus and attention to play at a championship caliber level.

    We all need to focus more. Eliminate chaos. Get organized. Say NO to distractions.

12. **Get MO-mentum going in your favor** (see WOW 6). In football or in any sport for that matter, momentum shifts are huge. You can feel them happen at different times in a ball game. Heck, even in the fourth quarter of that national championship game, Florida State, led by Jameis Winston, roared back from an 11-point deficit and ended up winning late in the ball game.

You are going to feel momentum shifts in football and in life. The key is taking advantage of momentum when it's in your favor and slowing it down or stopping it when it's going against you.

So how do you get MO-mentum going in your life? You become an action-taker. You become a "driver" and not a "passenger." You say YES to what you do want and NO to what you don't want.

As pastor Miles McPherson from the Rock Church says, "Getting MO-mentum in your life leads to MO-harmony, MO-happiness, MO-money, MO-everything . . . and not necessarily in that order."

Get "MO" in your life!

13. **Have a deep-seated purpose.** What is the purpose of playing the game of football? Or the purpose of a season? While you can argue that it's about winning championships and accolades, some coaches or organizations are just trying to claw out of the cellar of the league. Or to build character and confidence in players. Or to give kids from economically depressed areas or troubled home-lives hope for the future.

In life, we all need a purpose. I know my purpose is to inspire millions to greatness and create IMPACT everyday. That drives me. That empowers me. That wakes up my spirit every morning to utilize my God-given abilities to do good things in life and make a difference. But that's MY purpose.

WHAT'S YOURS?

Each of us has been blessed with different gifts. You just have to dig deep to find your gifts, use your gifts, share your gifts, and live your most profound purpose.

You see—**football IS like life**. Between playing the game for approximately 15 years, being a strength coach/trainer for high-level athletes for 21-plus years, and being a fan my whole life, I know this game. And I know what it has taught me about life. **Football and life go together.** Just like fathers and sons.

I watched Florida State eek out a close and exciting game over Auburn with my two boys beside me. One munching on peanuts and Cracker Jacks and watching the Goodyear blimp and the cheerleaders. The other intently watching the game he so desperately wants to play in the coming years. There is nothing better than moments like these.

Here's to the great game of football!

 **ACTION STEP**

Out of the "Thirteen Points," which ones most speak to you and how can you apply them to your life? Write them down, create a specific plan on how to accomplish them, work diligently to do so, and make it happen!

AND THEN SOME...
CREATE WOW NOW!!!

A respected colleague and friend of mine Pat Rigsby once told me, "You're the Tony Robbins of the fitness industry."

And while that's all fine and dandy and a compliment to a guy who absolutely loves the **IMPACT** Tony creates, my whole thing is— Why be confined to JUST the fitness industry?

When it comes to motivation . . . we ALL need it.

When it comes to inspiration . . . we ALL need it.

When it comes to discovering your deepest purpose, your deepest passion . . . we ALL need it.

You have heard me say before that is takes "**PASSION, PURPOSE, and IMPACT**" to create the life you desire.

And when it comes to creating maximum **IMPACT** in your **LIFE** and creating **WOW** . . . each and every one of us **NEEDS** that now.

So in this book, you have 52 inspirational WOW stories and lessons designed to get **your MIND and SPIRIT right**—right now. And if you go to www.ToddDurkin.com/WOWBook-AndThenSome, you'll find 8 more "**And Then Some . . . WOWS**," to help you keep that momentum going strong.

My friends, know that you are designed for **greatness. Greatness** is within each of you. Each and every one of you.

And in order to **BE GREAT**, that entails you **GOING DEEP**, doing some serious soul-searching, listening to that little "voice" in you guiding you to a place that scares you.

And if you keep hearing that "voice," that's a **SIGNAL**. Focus on the signal and eliminate all the "noise" around you. Let your **SPIRIT** be stirred and let your **SOUL** sing.

I have said for many years, **"Everyone has a life worth telling a story about . . . what's your story?"**

Your job is to craft up the most amazing life—and amazing story—you can ever imagine. Create **WOW** in your life. Make your life story **WOW-worthy** (heck, maybe even WOW #53 should be about YOU!)!

And if you don't like the life you are currently living, then **change** YOUR story.

It's going to take courage.

It's going to take **GUTS**. Commitment. Courage. Discipline. Focus. Sacrifice. Risk. Persistence. And a lot of hard work. And a ton of **FAITH**.

But you have to **BELIEVE** that you have BEEN blessed with a **deep PURPOSE** and that there is a special plan for you.

And while you may not know that plan right now, I can promise you one thing . . .

If you exercise and train consistently . . .

and you choose to eat healthy foods . . .

and you surround yourself with positive people . . .

and you read inspirational, motivational material, such as your WOW short stories, each and every day . . .

You WILL be more motivated.

You WILL be more inspired.

And you WILL be more empowered . . . than EVER before.

Keep striving for excellence, dreaming **BIG**, and creating **WOW** in your life!

Be STRONG and don't forget, **GET YOUR MIND RIGHT!!!**

Your WOW Coach,

Todd Durkin

ACKNOWLEDGMENTS

This book project has had so many people lift it up that it would be impossible to create a list of proper "thank-you's" to all involved. But here are a few of the people who have helped make this project possible. Thank you to all who have had a hand in its success.

My family—you all inspire me to be my best every day.

Melanie—you most of all deserve my thanks. It is you that makes it possible for me to serve my purpose. I love you very much.

Luke (13), my firstborn—you have changed me more than you can ever imagine. I just love watching you develop into such a fine, young gentleman. You are an exemplary student and one heck of an athlete. I know your hard work and practice is going to pay off. You have made me proud since day one, and I'm excited for what the future holds for you.

Brady (11)—you put such joy in my heart. I love how much we get each other, and you're one of my favorite people in the world to talk to! Your passion is unwavering, your light is so bright, and the future is yours to create whatever you so desire. Keep dreaming big—I'm so proud of you, young man. Thank you for being you.

McKenna (8), my "Daddy's little girl"—you just take my breath away when I look at you. Your smile, energy, personality, and tenacity are going to allow you to be a trailblazer in life. It has been so much fun to watch you mature into an athlete and a young girl, but you will always be my baby! Stay STRONG and show the world who you are. I love you. #MyEyesAdoreYou

Mom—you raised 8 kids. You sacrificed everything to put the family first. You taught me how to love, and you helped make me the man I am today.

Thank you for WHO you are and what you stand for. You're a blessing to the universe and have IMPACTED me more than you will ever know.

At the age of 82, not a day goes by that I am not grateful for your voice and smile. You epitomize STRONG and will always serve as a great source of INSPIRATION and LOVE to me.

My FQ10 family—

Rob Ewing, Director of Digital Media & Marketing—thank you for being so enthusiastic and energetic as you share your marketing prowess with the world. I am blessed to have you on my team.

Julie Wilcox, GM of Fitness Quest 10—thank you for helping to create the culture at the "Magic Kingdom" of all gyms. I couldn't do what I do without you. I think the world of you and can't imagine not having you in my life.

Amelianne Johannes, Director of Todd Durkin Enterprises—you helped spearhead the "back-end" of this book project and a whole bunch more. I appreciate you and your efforts.

My entire team of trainers, coaches, therapists, instructors, and "Directors of First Impressions" at Fitness Quest 10—you guys are the secret sauce that makes Fitness Quest 10 what I always dreamed it would be. Thank you for representing the best of the best.

All my clients, athletes, and members at Fitness Quest 10—I am lucky to do something that I love and call it "work." It is you all that contribute to making Fitness Quest 10 the most positive place in the world. And it's all of you that give us the opportunity to motivate, inspire, and do what we love—coaching you. I have learned more from you over the years than you've learned from me. I'm grateful for the opportunity to serve you.

The Todd Durkin Mastermind Group—For many years, I only shared my "WOWs" with the trainers/coaches in my Mastermind Coaching Group. And then it grew and grew . . . and grew. Thank you, Mastermind Team, for always inspiring me to be my best and for being the positive "life-transformers" that the world needs more of.

All the fans and supporters who have emailed, Tweeted, Facebooked, IG'd, or sent messages saying something to encourage and inspire me—I read all of them, and it's your messages that I receive daily that keep me inspired and motivated to deliver my life's purpose. Thank you.

Nancy Pile—my godsend editor who stayed on top of me and held me accountable with deadlines, so I could get this project finished. Thank you!

FINAL PRAISE

Most of all, I want to thank God for the words behind this book. God is the extraordinary power behind my words, and his spirit flows through me. It is through faith in the Father, Son, and Holy Spirit that I am able to live with such passion, be convicted of such purpose, and help others create impact. #Faith

Visit

www.ToddDurkin.com/WOWBook

for free tools and resources that
will help you create WOW in your life.

BRING WOW TO YOUR TEAM!

If you are interested in bringing Todd Durkin's inspiring and motivational messages to your team, company, and/or organization, contact Todd Durkin Enterprises at one of the following:

Phone: (858) 271–1171

Email: durkin@fitnessquest10.com

Online: www.ToddDurkin.com (You will find a complete list of keynotes and programs here.)

Twitter: @ToddDurkin

Instagram: @ToddDurkin

Facebook Page: Facebook.com/ToddDurkinFQ10

Sign up for Todd Durkin's free weekly "Dose of Durkin" at www.DoseOfDurkin.com.

Sign up for Todd Durkin's free monthly "TD TIMES" e-newsletter at www.ToddDurkin.com.

Additional bonuses, resources, exercises, and messages can be found at www.ToddDurkin.com/WOWBook.

BULK DISCOUNTS
AVAILABLE

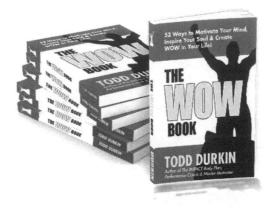

Order books in bulk at www.ToddDurkin.com/WOWBook

Ideal for:

✓ **Businesses with multiple teammates**

✓ **Leaders who want to inspire their teams**

✓ **Owners, Directors, or Executives**

✓ **Meeting or Event Planners**

✓ **Individuals who want to gift motivation & inspiration to family members, friends, or teammates**

✓ **Teachers, Professors, and Educators (Elementary School to Graduate School)**

TODD DURKIN
"CREATING WOW IN ALL ASPECTS OF YOUR LIFE."

Todd Durkin is available for speaking, coaching, and leadership training for businesses, conferences, organizations, and associations.

Please visit www.ToddDurkin.com to see potential topics, video clips, training resources, and other details on how Todd Durkin can create WOW for you and your organization.

ABOUT THE AUTHOR

Todd Durkin is an internationally recognized strength, speed, and conditioning coach, author, and speaker. He currently owns and operates Fitness Quest 10 in San Diego, California, which has been named a "Top 10 Gym in America" the past 5 years by *Men's Health*. In 2016, Todd was a featured trainer and finalist on NBC's *STRONG* produced by Dave Broome and Sylvester Stallone.

Growing up in a poor household and having witnessed his parents' divorce at a young age, Todd's outlets were sports and fitness. His early experiences fueled his passions that led him to land a college football scholarship as a quarterback and eventually a professional football career in Europe. His dreams of playing in the NFL were shattered after a serious back injury. During his recovery, Todd spent many years learning from training, rehabilitation, and healing gurus in Europe and the US while he honed his craft. This culminated in a training and bodywork methodology that has helped thousands of people get out of pain and improve performance.

Now, Todd has been awarded some of the industry's highest honors, which include being named one of America's "Top 100 Most Influential People in Health and Fitness" in the US. He is the Lead Training Advisor for Under Armour, and he has been named "Personal Trainer of the Year" by both IDEA and ACE. Additionally, Todd and his team earned the 2015 California Small Business of the Year Award, recognizing them as one of the top 120 businesses out of 3.3 million in the state of California.

Todd is the author of the *IMPACT! Body Plan*, a comprehensive plan to change body, mind, and spirit. He has appeared on *60 Minutes* and been featured on ESPN and the NFL Network and in *Sports Illustrated*, *Men's Health*, and the *Wall Street Journal*, among other outlets. Todd trains some of the top athletes in the world, including those in the NFL, MLB, MMA, and Olympics. This includes NFL MVPs, Super Bowl Champions and MVPs, Heisman Trophy Winners, Olympic and X-Game Gold Medalists, MMA World Champions, and many other champion athletes.

He lives by the words *passion*, *purpose*, and *IMPACT*. Todd has been married for 15 years to his wife, Melanie, and they reside in San Diego with their three kids, Luke, Brady, and McKenna.

Visit www.ToddDurkin.com for all information.

The Durkin Family
(L/R: Brady, Melanie, McKenna, Jersey, Todd, Luke)

Made in the USA
Lexington, KY
11 October 2016